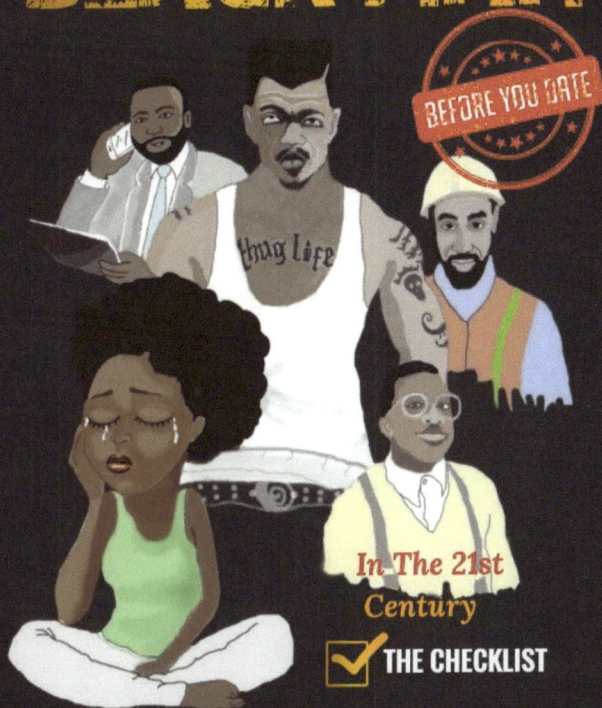

SISTAS PRE-QUALIFY A BLACK MAN IN THE 21ST CENTURY BEFORE YOU DATE

"STOP Dating Just MALES and
START Dating MEN!"

The Checklist

MR. WOLF

Table of Contents

Acknowledgments

I would like to thank one of my best friends, Queen Alena D. Jones Smith, for always encouraging me to write my book. You have always encouraged me through the years. I really appreciate your relentless positivity! You have always helped me to push forward in my ventures.

I would like to thank my best friend, Edwin Harper, who has also encouraged me to push forward in finishing these books in my mind and heart. You always encourage me to be the best that you know I can be. We have been through many trying experiences together, and we have remained friends. You are more of a brother to me than you know. I wish you much success in your marriage and raising your children as well as your business ventures.

I would like to thank my best friend Marshall Walker III for always supporting me in so many ways. I cannot even count them all! You have given me so much rich insight into the past. I appreciate the emotional support and comfort you have provided me in your own many ways! You are like a father to me, considering our 25-year age difference, and like a big brother also, depending on the situation. I love you no matter what you decide to do in the Golden Years of your life.

I want to thank my "cuzzbro" (cousin/brother), Jason Braxton, for always inspiring me with his endless love, support, and skills as a writer in his own right. I want to see your book soon, cousin. I love you.

I would like to thank another one of my best friends, Christopher Simmons, affectionately known as "CJ." You are one of my best friends. You are my business partner in so many ways and my accountability partner in the Black Community. You always support me in all positive Black ventures that I decide to take on; you are an example of what is possible in the Black Community. You have helped so many Black people with your great wisdom on "legal hustles" and carpentry in places only a tough person would go! You are a true brother in hard times! You are one of the hardest working Black Men that I know! Thank you, bro., I love you for that. You always inspire me.

I would like to thank Natascha Bodley, my last best friend, who has always seen the light in my tunnel and encourage me directly and indirectly as we learn different things about our individual journeys in this thing called life!

I would like to thank Dr. Chike Akua for his mentorship and teaching the Black and Brown children about their African roots in the school system. You inspired me and others worldwide to become authors and give our experience to our Black and Brown Communities who need our leadership! Keep up the great work my brother!

I would like to thank the countless number of sistas that I have met on this journey as well as friends, family, and associates through the years who remain nameless due to their privacy concerns...you know who you are! You have shared the most intimate details of your lives, which have given me part of my baseline understanding and wisdom within our Black Community of positivity, negativity, dysfunctional lifestyles, mixed with intense emotional trauma, hard work, hope, and resilience! Thank you all, and I hope to help set some of your offspring free to choose a better life by reading this information that took 35+ years to finally put together!

PREFACE

This book was difficult to write for so many reasons! I have been contemplating writing this book for the last 10years! Let me just state that for the record! I'm forced to tell you the truth, since you are not getting good advice from your circle judging by the rate of dysfunctional homes, we have today in our communities run mainly by single parent females/women. Listen, I am just a man who paid close attention and has studied my people over the past 35+years or so and discovered a *serious* pattern! I have asked the hard questions over the span of my life. Although not formally educated with a college degree in the European system of education, such as in Psychology or early child development, etc., I know that I have some of the answers through my extensive informal interviews in my life's journey in the belly of the beast of dysfunctional Black family life and hood environments! I can assist PRO Black/Afrikan and Afro-Latinas in solving some of our issues at the root by following this advice which I have laid out in this book. There are very calculated reasons why we don't have many good books, in my opinion, on how to navigate the mental complexities in this Americanized culture which makes it very difficult to rebuild our BLACK Communities from a more natural perspective! We have been wired incorrectly from birth in a society that does not promote healthy Black relationships between Black Men and Black Women. That is by design, my sistas!

Nowadays, sistas know extraordinarily little about what a real MAN *is,* compared to a just a grown Male! You don't know us at all. There is no "formal education" that you can get anywhere in America, or Western countries that I know of that will teach you the skills on effectively becoming a housewife, domestic partner, or that will help you acquire a man. You must also know how to keep him and sustain a "healthy" relationship with him, for the best years of your life with balance and understanding. In the old days prior to 1980's the Bible, Qur'an and mature older women had done that their entire lives! Today, social media is the teacher of our sistas and disgruntled older women who can't keep a good man to save their own lives, yet they teach! The question then remains…what if you don't follow any formal religion or don't have balanced parents at home, like so many of the youth today? You need sound guidance in a Modern World where people have turned away from religious or spiritual teachings in the sense that they rely on Google, Instagram, Facebook, Snapchat, Twitter, Tik-Tok, YouTube, and now OnlyFans.com for their guidance over religion and things of a spiritual nature! You think otherwise? This book is not about judging you in your belief systems. I just want to show you the basis of where the elders got their guidance on relationships in the 20th Century and prior to the age of Modern Technology and lifestyles! Just look online and see what your friends, family, and associates believe in and comment on in an average day on social media to prove my point! How does a man decide to treat you when he doesn't look to God as a judge for his actions? You need to prepare yourself! In my future book titled: 'Sistas Pre-Qualify A Black Man In The 21st Century Before You Date; Stop Dating Just Males and Start Dating Men! "The Blueprint;" I will break down the main types of guys you will meet on your journey called life, in a technology-driven world! Honestly, nobody really cares about what happens to Black people worldwide outside of our own people! They just do not want to really see the drama play out in their faces and affecting or infecting their lives in whatever bad things happen to us as a whole! Few if any, are going to write an effective book that will ultimately remove "other groups" from our Black pockets from a dating relationship perspective! Why should they? Here is what I mean. A thriving Black family would *derail* so many other economies! In a "hardcore" *capitalistic* society, like America, there must be a "lower class" and a *"scapegoat"* for it to work! Can you guess who got that title? Us! We must be honest with ourselves and realistic in our expectations for our future! Some will say to you...girl, we have so many choices, it doesn't matter what others think about you, you don't even need a Black Man! You can be anything and do anything that you want! This whole "cancel culture" is some B.S.! Look around and see the lifestyle of 50-year-old and up single Black/Brown women who don't have a man and who didn't become highly successful financially! If they are honest with themselves, they are not happy alone and they are struggling financially if not living with other women or family. Truth be told, if we didn't have so many modern conveniences that men have built in our society, they would be miserable and would come to terms with reality. Thanks America, for making most of our sistas delusional when it comes to financial and emotional security under 60 years old, with no decent husband in sight! If you take away the government support by removing sliding scale housing, employment, and financial resources allocated to our sistas, they would be very uneasy in a world run by men. The funny thing is...other non-Black women seem to think they need a decent to successful Black man. Yes, you need us too, so please stop with the social media rants! Sure, you can say the same thing about other non-Black men needing you, right? Sure, that happens, just at a much lower rate when it comes to marriage! Dating doesn't equal marriage to a man. Black women are not marrying men in record numbers. Most of our sistas want a Black Man only and will hold out to get one. You don't know how to choose though. I commend you on your loyalty to your own, yet you need training on what Men want from a

Woman and a lifetime companion. I am not trying to tell you that YOU are valued less, but yeah, overall, nobody will value our women as a group more than our own Black MEN. Yeah, I said that! We are not talking about emotions. We are talking about facts! If you disagree, then perhaps you do not realize there is also distinct differences between females and women. I will explain later.

Who Should Read This Reference Book

Here is who should read, re-read and study this checklist that I have laid out as a reference guide through my personal story and thousands of experiences in the Black and Brown communities! I hope you have the patience to open your mind and really soak up what I'm telling you! If you were raised by your mother alone without much input from a strong father figure, you need this book. If you were raised in foster care homes with some very unbalanced and maybe even non-black or brown parents, you need this book! If you were raised with a father and no mother present and your father spent all or most of his time working and not teaching you about guys, you need this book! If you come from a dysfunctional environment with either parent in which your father and or mother was abusive to you, and you want to date a balanced young or older man, you need this book! If your single mother talks in a negative way about men because your father or other guys abandoned you and her for whatever reason, you need this book! If you don't know who your father was or is, and your mother has not provided a good man as a father figure for you, you need this book! If you are a single mother with children in your home and you want to date again, you need this book! If you are a young female from 14yrs old and up…in high school who insists on dating and or having sex with males earlier than you should, you need this book! Yes, I said it! You need to know what you are getting into! You need to read this book. I don't approve of you having sex before 21yrs old and or while you are still in high school. I also don't approve of you having unprotected sex with anyone you are not married to as well! I'm your dad, your uncle, and your brother...saying NO! Just for the record! You see, I know some mothers will say that I'm giving you the green light to do so by saying that. I assure you that I'm not, but what I know is this...if you want to do it...you will do it and without your mama's consent! Most parents have maybe not figured out that you are more influenced these days by your friends than your parents, especially if you spend small amounts of quality time with them. My goal is to *educate* them (youth) on what could and likely will happen based on that path, especially not having a *strong* and *balanced* father figure who is present and aware who *knows how* to *teach* you male vs. man psychology! The best thing you can do as a *single* parent is to *educate* them on the *consequences* because they don't have a clue of the really bad things that potentially await them right around the corner unless you, as a parent, have already set a bad example! This may require you to take them to meet other females and women who have made these very same mistakes to show them what their lives could look like on that path, with accountability in mind, not just guy bashing! If you messed up, then they really need an outside perspective to show them the way. Do this whole "birds and bees" talk thing *before* they reach high school! Let's say around 6yrs old, then 10yrs old, another more detailed sexual education discussion around 13 years old before they get to high school! You don't have to be graphic, but if they have a phone (bad idea) or their friends have a smartphone and or access to the internet without parental controls, get started ASAP!

The others that should read this book are those between 14 to 45 years old who still have the *ability* NOT to *pre-judge* a Black man for the damage they have received over the years from those of the opposite sex, whether from their father figure, uncle, brother, cousin or any other Black male they chose to date! I say that because if you have been wounded and *can't* get past it with meditation and or prayer, please get help from an older woman mentor who has the results you seek, etc. Get some professional help from a therapist; if nothing else, preferably a Black woman married happily to a Black man! Sis, without counseling, *honest self-examination,* and *personal development*, then respectfully, there is not much that will *change* in your situation! Anybody who tells you that it will is doing you a disservice and lying to you! God got you, right? I heard that one also. It's *true,* and then in some cases, it is used as an excuse not to do the work! Well, I'm here to tell you God got us all, but low self-esteem from trauma, etc., isn't going to be solved with just praying! I can hear the religious older women now (straight face). Well, you must know, God loves me also, so should you! (smile) Here is a message for my Christian folks! "FAITH *without* works is DEAD!" That means it takes work with those *many* prayers you are sending up for anything meaningful to change! Get focused now! I know too many older Black females and women who are still living out their childhood and past relationships that robbed them of their *youth* through their daughters, nieces, etc. They trust and hope for a good Black man in their lives without putting real effort into their own personal development and fitness! Some of them go to church several times a week! They are angry or sad, depending on how things worked out! I hear the same things all the time! "If I ONLY knew, what I know now!" "If I would have done this or that!" "Why didn't I just leave earlier?"

Listen, I respect discipline and patience. I have sacrificed the best years of my life NOT to make the same mistakes that my parents, relatives, friends, and associates made. I love my future family so much that I wanted to make sure I knew that I was past the dysfunctional parts of my life. I prayed a lot also! It took 20+yrs of active personal development to get a handle on myself and figure out the issues within myself. Have you started? What is your current age? How much time do you think you have to get this right? I'm still not perfect, but nobody is, including the expert Psychologists some people pay big money to, to discuss their many problems!

Most people ignore their issues until it reaches a peak, and this generally happens when they have exhausted all mental, social, physical and financial resources and vices (alcohol, marijuana, cocaine, heroin, meth, pills, homelessness, incarceration wakes some up also, etc.) and come full circle past 40yrs old! Some people die with those *unresolved* issues. Mission accomplished! The powerful people in the dominate society are winning so far. They are the ones who have put in place the systematic racist environment we live in, effectively helping you drain the best years of your life struggling with dysfunctional relationships and not building a legacy! You have just enough time to procreate the next dysfunctional generation, flawless victory for them! Stop this madness!

Some sistas try to stay so busy with their career or children's activities so much they don't have to think about the mental wars raging on within them. They pray and expect things to get better all the time without *real* action. Things will not change for you that way! You will just *likely* bring children into this world and keep it going for the next generation to figure it out on their own or taking your bad advice about guys. It is very foolish, to say the least, to *gamble* with your future legacy! Please get the help you need! Don't look for a guy to make you happy. You must be content with who you are if you are indeed mature. Do you really know who you are? What is your purpose on this earth? It can't just be to raise children alone and then die an old maid or grandmother gossiping on social media about the next drama-filled relationship post! If you are solid mentally, physically, and spiritually (not necessarily religious) on your own, great! Now get a partner who can add to your life. Here is where I come in. I'm here to shorten your "learning curve" with the opposite sex! I'm going to show you how to be more effective if you *allow* me to give you a hand.

I always tell sistas who need a hand all the time. *"Be part of your own rescue!"* If I throw you a life preserver...**TAKE IT AND HOLD ON TIGHT!**

DEDICATION

I dedicate this book to my mother, who sacrificed her "best years" in life to the wrong person because of not really knowing how to choose a mate! You were a great example of what a mother should be to her young children. You just didn't have the best options, growing up in a small town, to draw from, to make better decisions in the dating game with only a limited knowledge on relationships with the opposite sex outside of marriage. How could you win with so many negative variables at that time once you stepped out of your secure home, relying on prayer alone? You couldn't win nor can many other sistas without Modern Day wisdom for the 21 Century dating arena!

I dedicate this book to my maternal grandmother. Big Mama, you showed me through your example what true strength is in a woman, even lacking adequate basic education. You were a real woman, wife and mother! You were kind, sweet, gentle and physically and mentally tough. You were a good wife and midwife who knew how to heal us all through your natural remedies passed down from previous generations of women. I love you Big Mama, and I miss you!

I would also like to dedicate this book to my 1st niece, Aysia, who I hope will allow me to assist her in her education on choosing a man and not just dating males for the best years of her young life. Niecy, I love you and I want to see you win in a troubling world full of corruption and deceit at every turn! You need to know how to conduct yourself as a young lady, despite what social media tells young adults is cool and acceptable!

Finally, I would like to dedicate this book to any unborn or future daughters I may father. I want them to have this information in case I don't live to see them grow up and have a dating life of their own. Baby, I love you and want to see you win in life with a decent and balanced Black Man to continue the legacy of greatness that I want to start with my own family!

INTRODUCTION

Everyone has their own opinion on what they think is best, based on their experiences. I'm not any different in that regard. My question is this, though, how many mentors do you have or know of with a personal background interviewing and researching real people for over 35 years? I'm talking about real reformers who have survived their dysfunctional upbringing and thrived with their mental health, then come back and try to save others? Some people surround themselves with others who will tell them what they want to hear. Don't do that. You can't grow like that! When you love the people in your circle, it truly is difficult to tell them the truth because you know the pain it will cause them, yet you must do so with tact and love if possible! Are you willing to sacrifice blood, sweat, and tears to help your Black community? Most people will not go so far; not even give 20% of their time. As soon as they experience emotional pain, they leave whoever they were attempting to assist. You see, it is easy to give empty advice when you never experienced that type of severe pain outside of your own issues, and you can just go home when you get tired of dealing with somebody else's issues. Imagine when you are in a relationship, and you get that uneasy moment when you realize this guy is NOT the one, and he is going to give you more grief than you can really handle over the next 3-6 months and beyond! Time to leave, right? Not so easy for those who are suffering internal trauma from their childhood and early adulthood who want to feel some sort of security, love, affection and appreciation. Most people don't grow past their childhood trauma "alone" in my experience.

I've been in great pain for not sharing what I know is true all these years! I didn't feel the western cultured Modern Day Black women were ready to hear the truth. We can't keep playing this game anymore sis! It kills our future to not be counseled or corrected in a society that makes just about anything OK for you to do. Do you really think there won't be long-term consequences of poor judgment with the opposite sex that you may never recover from emotionally and or financially? Seriously? You can't date like guys date and get a desirable result long-term! Some would-be mentors get caught up in the emotions of it all and get overwhelmed and give up without really having an effective process to assist those in need of relationship support. We need to calculate if the person we are attempting to help is really within reach by our hands, by getting some background information up front first! How many of those who counsel you have lived in the "hood" for most of their lives and survived with their mental health intact; enough to come back for others and teach them how to free themselves of social bondage? How many of them know how to win in the dating game with men? I'm not sure of the ratio of "street" qualified professionals, based on what I have read so far and seen with my own 2 eyes. I'm not so confident in what they know! What I see in this society is that people come out of the hood and then go live "across the tracks" so to speak, with people that don't look like them. They live in the most affluent areas and put their children in better schools and try to forget everything bad that happened to them or they saw happened to others. I understand why they leave and do not look back or go back. Well, in my life, I've tried to understand that trauma from an alternative perspective. You see, I stayed close to my people because I wanted to help those I loved and who look like me! I realized that if every Black person keeps forgetting about their people who are struggling, nothing will change, and as we get older, the environments that we would like to see changed will remain the same. You know the people in the dominant society are not going to assist you in the problems they gave your people, right? I hope you realize that by now, especially after a Donald Trump presidency and all the countless lynching of Black/Brown men! It is a great task to ask someone to go back to the hood when most of the people you knew came from highly dysfunctional families. They see no way out of their living situations, so they move. Well, I'm going to give you an insider's view of the very predatory mindset of the males vs. men argument. If these people with Doctorate degrees are so educated and smart, why hasn't the tide turned in the places where we live? Could it be they haven't practiced where we have these issues with effective plans to combat the narrative and negative training our sistas are receiving from scorned Black women in our society based on the bad choices they made in guys? Could it be that they don't see any real money involved in positive Black community building? Personally, I know you can leave the hood, but you must go back to visit and teach to make lasting changes! You should deploy your experience and understanding to help others who must be there right now. Could these so-called mentors of our sistas be focused on the wrong things? I have some answers, but the answers are simple, yet hard to swallow for our sistas who already love or lust for guys who they think are men or thought of as men when they started having relations with them! Have you ever asked yourself what would happen if the Black communities were equally strong and self-sufficient outside of allowing the people in the dominant society to control the narrative and the state of their communities where they live by taking ownership of their own narrative and education? The keys are in the FAMILY foundation.

Nobody, and I mean nobody, is going to be concerned about solving the Black communities' biggest issues beyond our own people. They have been instigating negativity in the school system that teaches our youth that your people started out as slaves and with predominately non-Black teachers. The media and entertainment industry promote negative rhetoric about the Black Communities. Thus, they will not contribute positively to the growth of our Black Communities. We must tackle this issue, with testicular fortitude going forward with Black MEN!

The breakdown through all these things and the slave culture given to us for 500 years and reinforced with the War on Drugs policies and school to prison pipeline over the last 50years has ripped Modern Day Black families apart! This makes things much harder to calculate, with those who are too lazy to read history and its effects! There are direct correlations between these periods and what you see today with our broken homes. In my opinion, the miseducation of Americans, especially Black/Brown Americans through school systems, lamestream media outlets, and slut culture entertainment is the most powerful subjugation tools in the U.S. against Black people! Everything negative is promoted as the fingerprint of American Slave Culture. You don't believe that? No problem. Just do some traveling, and you will see what people think they know about Black people in other countries. It is mainly based on the entertainment promoted worldwide from the TV, news, and social media outlets. This is what other people believe we are. They don't know much about America; they only know what they see on TV, social media over the internet, and the lamestream media outlets.

I have traveled to several different countries, and I have been on 4 different continents to date; it is always the same narratives! They think they know how we are due to America's broadcast to the world that the Black Community is dangerous, violent, stupid, and irresponsible about their family dealings. I had to debunk that constantly, and I would hear, you're not like the other Black Men that we have seen or see on TV, etc. They often say that our Black women are so aggressive and masculine. Brazilian women told my cousin who lives in Brazil, that our women compete with the men too much! WOW! The narrative is very strong against us. I just give them the smirk like, REALLY? It is so tiring sistas! Let's change that viewpoint not for them, but for all conscious Black people. Let's lead by example.

When I say Sistas, I do include Afro-Latinas and any other sistas that have an "Afro-"in front of their group description and mixed-race Pro-Black sistas because I know they face similar problems. We are prime targets for the negative stereotypes in just about every country in the world, including African countries, thanks to the United States' negative promotions! I know you may likely choose not to listen to my very honest advice, but don't complain when White women and Asian women date the best of our Black men in our communities in the future. They will see the good in Black men that possibly some of our wounded sistas will not. I apologize to you for the guys in your life that have failed you. I'm sorry that you didn't have a good father figure in your life or a good Black man by your side initially. I advise you to seek therapy if you need it after being emotionally damaged by some male in your current life or past. You must feel good about yourself mentally first, and don't expect a man to fix your self-esteem! I would advise you to seek counseling from another sista who does that as her business with successful results as a therapist! Just make sure she has a good Black man herself if she is promoting marriage and then when you are ready to tackle the dating scene, refer to my checklist to give you an edge in your life that most of your single sista circle will not have! I may also suggest meditation while you work on yourself. We have been jumping from trauma related to trauma-filled or drama-filled relationships and wondering why the wound never heals. We must first address our mental and physical health, then tackle getting to know the opposite sex part. We must stop creating dysfunctional families, and this will be my contribution. I can't wait to break this down for you in the pages of this book. Read this with an open mind and heart, and I promise you that you will meet and date more men and perhaps find the one for you!

I will tell you a few things about yourself and your responsibilities. You have the power to decide your attitude, submissiveness, physical fitness, sexual partner(s), and or guy(s) you decide to date. I can see some of your faces right now, so let me just say this. "Submission does not equal oppression!" So, if you are upset or outright angry, don't blame Black men for your poor choices! I love you enough to tell you the truth. You don't know how to choose a MAN. I want to SCREAM that to the mountains for some sistas! Highly intelligent in everything else, but less than adequate in choosing a MAN these days! Likely, the damage you have faced came at the hands of weak Males and not strong Black MEN. Reading and studying this information as a "reference" or guide will give you more options than you would ever have otherwise, with application and discipline! I'm going to lay out for you what you need to know that most of your girlfriends who haven't read this book don't know. You decide how you want to implement this strategy or *gamble* like you have been doing so far. I know this information will end up in the right hands eventually, if not at first!

I know EXACTLY why Black Males and Men date outside of their own group also. Some of it is because they are COONS, who don't want to be Black themselves and would rather be White or etc....and the OTHERS because of the emotional support, RESPECT and nurturing they receive elsewhere. I know...I know...easy for them to do, when the "other" women don't have the issues we inherited, right? Well, guys don't think that way! Don't get mad about it. EDUCATE YOURSELVES AND START TO WIN! You can and should stop one thing, though. STOP listening to Black females who don't have a good and strong Black man! This is your first step. I don't care if it is your mama, grandmother, auntie, cousin, friend, colleague, or associate! If they don't have a PRO Black Man as a husband or significant other, they can't really give you adequate good advice on how to acquire or keep one! Even if a guy doesn't have a solid relationship with a Black woman, he doesn't have to ever lose in finding a good wife. There are plenty to choose from worldwide. A man can always find a good woman to be by his side. Not all women can say that. Sounds harsh? It's reality! Unfortunately, in society, women have a shelf life to the opposite sex due to instincts about having children, etc. I can't stop you from being angry about it. What you can do is use that information to propel your efforts forward in the right direction. Disagreeing with me will not help you after you turn 30yrs+ with no good prospects, and you will be wondering why. IF you are 40 – 50 years old, you should have a laser beam focus on what you are doing to change that course. You will have to take drastic measures if you let yourself go physically. I can still assist you with some things, but I can't make any projections about your results, until you hit the gym! Even older men want women 20+ years their junior, who is submissive and nurturing, with a decent to great shape! You can still get in the game if you are in decent to tip-top shape and you are middle-aged with somewhat positive results if you use my guidelines below. The decision is yours to make. Be realistic in your expectations of physical and financial attractiveness of a man that chooses you, comparable to your perceived sexual market value.

Let's get into "THE CHECKLIST" for every group of women with real dating opportunities and how to proceed for the best possible results for you and those you lead through example!

CHAPTER 1:

SOCIALIZED PROGRAMMING

Let us be direct for a minute. If you are not a light brown sista or light-bright, almost White sista...Western societies look down on you the most! They encourage "colorism" in many ways; to ensure the conflicts within Black people. You notice who gets the best jobs when it comes down to equal skills or close to it? Most jobs don't hire the best qualified person. They hire somebody they know, like and trust or is "culturally acceptable" to their disposition! Skin color and ethnic group play a major role in that for us, in a very Whitewashed society. Dating is an interview for a job also. You know I am telling you the truth, and brainwashed Black males buy into that mindset, unfortunately! It comes from a society built on slavery. This is all reinforced by everything you see "seemingly" successful in entertainment and negative in the news media. Here is a book that all Black and Brown people need to read, whether you think it does apply to you or not, called "Post Traumatic Slave Syndrome" by Dr. Joy Degruy. This sista is amazing in her research! I have seen her speak in person. The background and history of American Slavery is very deep, and we are all infected by it even to this day! Yes, if you are a Hispanic, it affects you and infects you also, whether you know it or not, some if not most of you have roots in African ancestry as opposed to Europeans like the Portuguese or Spaniards! This is history, and you must remember one thing about American culture whether you are living in it here or reading this from another country! America is the leader of the world right now... and what America promotes to the world...directly or indirectly, the other countries buy into that mindset as well! If America promotes brown and dark skin as inferior, then that is what society will adopt! Hey, I never said it would be easy living here as Brown people, and damn sure not for Black people worldwide! Don't let that be an excuse not to be your best version of yourself though! This is something you will have to come to terms with at an incredibly young age. Research the "The Doll Test" on YouTube. I just want you to know that this information on the Black population is needed throughout the world because America's pull is strong! As a result, you are at the bottom of the *desirable* dating pool by society's standards. Some other races have *private talks* to their family members about NOT bringing home a Black or Brown girl for *serious* dating or marriage. Oh yeah...I know personally that these things happen. Some Black parents even make comments about bringing home a dark-skinned sista, and if you are a Latina...no Moreno o Negros en la familia! In Africa, women are bleaching their skin to appear more beautiful from a Western cultural perspective, risking skin cancer, death, etc.! Sistas are putting on wigs, wearing hair hats and ridiculous looking weaves that guys sit back and talk about behind closed doors and online chat rooms discussing how stupid they think you look! Many of our continental African people who have not traveled to the Western countries have been taught to reinforce this madness about white skin and dark skin color by what they see online, TV, and entertainment as what is acceptable in America as the beauty standard around the world! Things are changing, but not fast enough for you to have so many great options without major guidance on how to navigate the system before you decide to date a guy! I am not saying these things to hurt you because I love you! I say this so you can get your mind right and focus on building your own communities with some worthy brothers!

You need to know what you are looking at to win in this dating game, which from my experience, my interviews and independent studies, 90 % of you don't! You could go on this journey on your own like many have decided to do yet look at the number of single parents in the Black and Brown communities. Traveling the country where Black/Brown people live, you meet many women with children but no man present. The younger affluent Black sistas are focusing on their careers until their mid to late 30s, thinking they got all the time in the world to find a good husband! A U.S. Census Bureau report in the past 4 years showed that Black men are taking White wives at twice the rate of Black Women. Other reports show that 93% of Black women married Black men. Listen, I hate to get into all these stats because it really means little to most sistas who are dating on emotions and not facts, with whoever makes them feel special and loved at the time!

You can do your own research if you are a nerd for numbers. The changes are significant in comparison to prior to the 1960's. If you are a conscious person...just go to where most Black people live, you will see the effects of fatherless children. Talk to your local teachers to see who has a dad at home or is involved with the children. The pattern is set in motion! Some statistics have stated that as much as 70% of Black women will never get married or have a real committed man in their lives! Look it up, no need to list it here. These are easy to find. This dysfunctional game has been in motion before we were born, and it has just gained momentum in the 21st century! For example, there is something you might find remarkably interesting about the studies in human behavior. Slaves were experimented on as well as animals in relationship trials. They were both taught how to respond to stimulus in a way that befitted the controller of the resources! That's heavy...you may not be mentally ready for this history lesson! You need to research Human Behavioral Science with B.F. Skinner. Also, look up Ivan Pavlov and look up his experiment called *Pavlov's Dog* on YouTube; if you seriously want to disagree with me...then continue here, and you will see! (In My Morpheus voice from The Matrix movie) "Do you think that is air you're breathing?" Let me remind you also that he (Pavlov) was born in the 1800s, and before that, we had almost 300 years of slavery in American culture in which slave behavior was studied, and the data gathered on how Black people respond to certain trauma, like removing the father from the home as the leader, protector and forcing the woman and children to rely on Massa, the White slave master! Look up "The Willie Lynch Letter". Please get Dr. Joy DeGruy's book and read it! It is a masterpiece of history! What does all of this have to do with Black men? Let me tell you. I have figured out how to help you navigate the duds from the studs, so to speak, with my 35 years + experience studying our people and how they make decisions! We are in major trouble, and I am not sure how much you understand, but our very existence in American family life structure and worldwide, hangs in the balance of what you do, with what I teach you! If we do not start taking care of the main problems within our communities as a UNIT, there will remain only negative stereotypes of Black men and women. The propaganda might prove TRUE for the majority... in a noticeably short period after the strongest and wisest of us have gone in the Baby Boomer and Generation X generations! I just want to give you a mere example of the type of science that is going on behind the scenes of your lives! We are just merely *existing* or *surviving* when we should be thriving later in our adulthood as a community, not just individuals! If you do not direct your life in a positive direction, someone else will always be willing to direct you, unfortunately, in the direction that will not benefit you and your community!

HIGH SCHOOL AND BEYOND
WILL BE VERY TOUGH

You are on the sexual market whether you are there as a willing participant or as clueless as Bambi in the forest! You have males and men with very primal instincts tracking your every move around you! Once a female reaches high school, things speed up at an intense pace from males to men observing you in different environments once you leave home. If you are above average looking or above average body, it is even at a feverish pace, which will make some very fearful! Sistas need security within the society that men built, down to the family head, your future husband, if you are blessed to acquire one.

Chapter 2:

MY STORY

"Life Lessons"

PILLOWS - Body Language, Verbal and Sexual

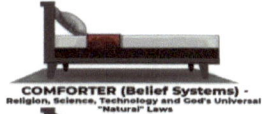

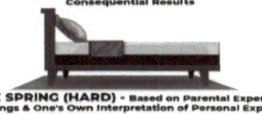

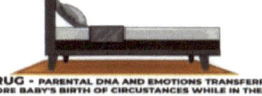

COMMUNICATION STYLE

COMFORTER (Belief Systems) - Religion, Science, Technology and God's Universal "Natural" Laws

THE REPRESENTATIVE

BEDDING - Style, Dress Code and Class

Physical Appearance

MATTRESS (SOFT) - Positive Future or Consequential Results

CHOICES & DECISIONS

BOX SPRING (HARD) - Based on Parental Experiences, Teachings & One's Own Interpretation of Personal Experiences

CHARACTER

BED FRAME - Pre-Existing At BIRTH, Human Subconscious Connection toward Survival, Nature & A HIGHER POWER

SPIRITUALITY

RUG - PARENTAL DNA AND EMOTIONS TRANSFERRED BEFORE BABY'S BIRTH OF CIRCUSTANCES WHILE IN THE WOMB

ENVIRONMENTAL

©2021 MR. WOLF

"WHEN YOU MAKE YOUR BED, YOU MUST LAY IN IT!"

There is an old saying from early as I remember all the elders in the Black Community would state. **"When you make your bed, you must lay in it!"**

I never knew how great that advice was, until I became a disciplined Man looking back on my life and that of people I have met along the way.

Sista as you experience the trials and tribulations of your dating life and possibly marriage, you must learn how to be accountable for your own actions, by evaluating your past and present decisions. Be very careful of the things you accept and reject since you will suffer or benefit by your own code you adapted along the way. The world is full of dysfunctional people and if you don't understand your own makeup, it's going to be very difficult to choose a man appropriately!

I grew up in a dysfunctional and Christian household like many of you reading this book, and if you are over 40 years old for the most part. How can one mix the 2? Well, let me tell you it was quite difficult! To even make matters worse, we were quite poor! You see, I grew up in the deep south, and we were poor even by those standards in a small town! My father became an alcoholic, and he smoked cigarettes in the house daily. He went out with his friends and uncles and got drunk on the weekends following a payday!

On the other hand, my mother was a God-fearing Christian and tried her best to keep the peace! To no avail! My father had anger issues because he had a difficult childhood himself, and as early as I remember, he took that anger out on the family, worst of all on my mother! He worked physically hard jobs! He had a dysfunctional upbringing coupled with the stress of systematic racism weighed heavily on his mind all the time! He gave us hell in my family house! My mother was a beautiful woman, a light-skinned sista with natural hair! We called them in the south "yella bone" or "red bone" women. We loved our brown to dark-skinned sistas also. Don't get it twisted! I just want to give you an image of what I endured, so you know that I know this life well and why you must listen from a MAN's perspective! Think for a moment, if this didn't happen to you, imagine you were my mother or even worse happened. Imagine you don't know the history of your prospective mate, and he was similar in character to my father or worse! My father sent my mother to church with us on some Sundays with sunglasses on her face to hide the black eye he gave her because he was drunk on that previous Friday night to Saturday night after a bad week at work! He was working under the harsh racist White man's rule, and he hated it! He talked about it constantly when he came home. It consumed his mind daily! Every other weekend he would come home off a binder with his best friend or a night out with his uncles, etc., looking to vent or fight. Sometimes they would either come over, which was rare; he didn't like anybody around my beautiful mother! Sometimes we would go to their homes, and someone would say something to my mama (flirting) or give too much eye contact to her that he thought was not cool. Instead of checking them about flirting, he would get upset with my mother, and we would then go home to his violent tantrum where he expressed his discontent! What do you expect when alcohol is heavily consumed in large or small groups with the opposite sex? My mother never did anything disrespectful toward my father with other men. She didn't really drink and didn't smoke either. She just smiled normally like a good host, and she was non-confrontational. I watched her closely. She never did much to enrage him. He just was a bitter guy because he wasn't where he wanted to be in life. Living with my father was tough most of the time because he lacked self-control with his tongue; his hands and feet expressed his anger from unresolved dysfunctional childhood memories fueled by alcohol and current racism. I give him some credit "specifically" because he did take on some of the responsibilities to feed, teach and clothe us for a short term which deserves some recognition. He never apologized to us for his behavior; he just made excuses. I thank God I had other solid men in my family to show me what he could not. Still to this day, my father is alone. He never re-married after they finally divorced. Thank God for that! No female or woman should get married to or have a domestic partnership with a guy without a good examination of his parental upbringing and his present mindset and lifestyle! You would never know my father's anger if you met him at a store or other venue. You think you know a guy? The signs are always there if you are trained to pick up on the cues. I sound crazy to some of you right now, and I know it. You don't know the male species well at all. You don't realize the danger you put yourself in by the looseness of your tongue. Some of you think because you win an argument that you are tough and strong. Let me just tell you, you can never beat a guy at being masculine. What I mean is for a side note. I have seen women being very disrespectful to a guy, and he is just a male, and then that guy would go out and get her on drugs or leave her somewhere where somebody else would take advantage of her, etc. There are many so-called, "strong Black women" in the grave today or dumped in a body of water, put there by a guy they once had a sexual relationship with and or marriage. Masculine males are very calculating when dealing with masculine female energy vs. feminine energy. He doesn't see you as a masculine woman psychologically, he sees you as a female competitor, not a companion, and there is a difference! If you challenge a guy, just ask yourself, what would he do, if those same words and attitude came from a male? True feminine energy doesn't challenge masculine energy, it balances it. BOOM! You are not ready for that talk, yet! (smile) I will get into that in my next book. You are a challenge to his authority in a way that he feels triggered to show his power. This is a mistake on your part if you are a masculine female. There are so many things you don't calculate in a relationship with a guy. You never win long-term when you are dealing with just a Male because he is only concerned with his needs not yours. Masculine females who want to date men never win long-term. Yet I digress. Back to my story.

My dad was a product of his upbringing and environment. Just imagine, they got married in their early 20s, and my mother was a virgin! They only dated maybe 3 months or so before they got married. She was loyal to my father to a fault! Hard core Christians don't believe in leaving their husbands or divorce except under extreme circumstances. My mother really was about that life! She was beautiful, humble, supportive, nurturing, hardworking, and submissive to my father's weak leadership. She was still called all sorts of names like stupid bitch or ho and physically slapped and beaten and mentally abused by him. I wanted to kill my father for a long time! I probably would have done it too, but my mother finally left for good and took us with her! Until this day, I don't associate with guys who beat their females/women. We could NEVER be friends! My mother knew that this would eventually catch up to him, with his young boys growing stronger every day. The crazy part is this, he wasn't all bad (hard to believe [smirk]) ...but the things I saw him do as a child created the dysfunctional example that my entire *immediate* family lives with to this day! I was so angry it consumed me for many years after I became an adult. My closest friends would encourage me to make peace with my father, so one day, I flew to the South approx. in the year 2011 where he is and had a 3-hour real talk with him about my upbringing, and the results of that conversation were staggering to my mental health and future! I forgave my father because I realized his upbringing in that conversation was not his fault, and he was merely acting out the anger he felt as a child from seeing what his father did in his home after returning to society after much killing in warfare in the military. That talk changed my life for the better! The weight on my heart was lifted, and I felt inner peace for the first time!

BETTER OPPORTUNITIES IN CALIFORNIA

My story isn't uncommon in the hood! I have met others that have endured much worse! Let's analyze my mother's future dating experience after leaving my father. Finally, my mama moved us to California. She was now single with 4 children in her late 30s. Serious dating was tough, and I watched my mother's journey along with her other single friends looking for a "Christian" man to marry. With 1 young toddler boy, 2 teenage boys, and 1 teenage girl in the house, my mother showed great discipline! She NEVER brought any dates home. She never had sex with any other guys either. I knew her belief system. She waited until she got married again. I didn't tell you all of that, to say that is what you should do! I'm merely telling you what young children SEE you doing or NOT doing makes a difference in how they choose their mates for relationships in their future! Your choice of a guy for long-term companionship, from domestic partnership to marriage, is ultimately important to your well-being beyond if he is rich and or how good he looks! An able-bodied male with no ambitious to work, provide for his wife, children and better himself, needs to be left alone, PERIOD!

40+ years later from my childhood, I can see the emotional crumbs of a dysfunctional upbringing with no reform, with bad parenting and sibling rivalry wars raging around the Black communities in the past 50+ years after the civil rights movement. Just look at my family, 4 children with different negative effects of their upbringing.

I tell you some of the most intimate details of *some* of my experiences to let YOU know that I'm secure in my truth; to help sistas avoid the traps of modern society with more freedom with technology and choices as mates! The game hasn't changed, though, just the wrapping! You will be lost in the sauce if you are taking seriously the advice of women who have NOT been happily married for 20+ years, and you ONLY are listening to angry, scorned women who sacrificed their youth to just male counterparts. I KNOW DYSFUNCTION in our Black Community well! I also KNOW how to avoid it and how to rebuild your mind from it. Choose wise counsel! This book is my attempt to save some sistas from a life of misery and hopelessness! If you are past your youth at the time of reading this book and or giving up on finding a good Black man, then you can give this gift to the young ones still in the game of dating and choosing a life partner. You must choose, though! I can't do that part for you. I can give you a bird's-eye view of what your life will look like based on what type of guy you like to date or choose to father your children! Do not even waste your time with dating books because it's pointless, in my opinion! You only need to know a *few things* about a guy in the beginning. I'm here to teach you that. After that, being *ignorant* can't be your excuse when you decide to be with a guy! I don't care what your age is. A leopard doesn't change its spots! Those spots are well defined once it's physically mature, knows how to hunt, and knows what it likes to eat. If you meet a guy over 25 years old, he is who he is! The late GREAT Maya Angelou said it best when she stated, "When someone shows you who they are, believe them the first time!" A guy has subconsciously decided on what type of person he is going to be by age 25. For the rest of his life, he is learning through practice to be just another grown male, bad guy, an average man, good man, or great man! Get that through your head! Another reason why young sistas should date older men, your chances are better at finding a man who could sustain any children in that union. If you say you want a real man, you need the details that I'm going to give you later in this book. Guys are simple and we are not going to change much from that age! He is merely honing his skills on his individual path. Take it or leave it! Just don't make excuses for yourself. Women choose & males lose. PERIOD.

PROTECT YOUR LEGACY WITH GOOD DECISIONS!

You should never bring guys home to meet your children unless he is serious and with the proper screening. You want to be intimate with a guy? Go to his place (no children) or get a motel/hotel. Children shouldn't know your business like that. I remember that to this day, and that is why I expect more from women when they have little children at home. Sex between consenting adults, no problem. Do your thing. I'm just saying, don't bring dudes to your place with your children! They don't need to be in your business. Another notable mention...this is how children get molested and raped or even end up dating much older females/males of yours, on the low. Trauma from childhood doesn't go away. It's even worse when your parent is involved!

Some of your children have been touched by *your* male associates who you thought were interested more in you, and you might not even know it! They might turn out to like your 14 – 21-year-old daughter instead or even younger. Yeah, the child who doesn't have a real dad in their lives. The one who is lacking a father figure, uncle, or older man cousin at the time. The one with low self-esteem. The one who doesn't really know that some attention from males is not good attention befitting a minor or young-minded girl or female by most standards! The young sista with no man coverage or protection in her family!

FAMILY TRAINING

Look at my mother, for example, she was *naive* with the opposite sex, but she wasn't stupid! She had class. Do you know why she had class? She was raised by one of the few stable couples in my entire family on both sides! She was the youngest of 8 children! My Big Mama sent her to live with my great aunt and uncle because she had her hands full, so to speak. They were a solid couple and solid individually! They showed her how to be a lady; they taught her to be classy and hardworking. My great aunt couldn't have children of her own, so it was easy for her to assist her sister by raising her niece. I'm not sure if my mother realized it at the time; she gained a great example of how to be a lady from one of the best!

You see, she had great training on being a real lady. We don't see that type of training being passed down as much anymore. How did she fail? She was beautiful and well trained in womanhood and wifely duties. Now she was divorced and back in the single crowd like many of you reading this book. She failed because she did not know how to choose a man. She relied heavily on advice from other women besides the aunt and uncle that raised her. "He is a Christian and believes in God," some said. I'm telling you that it matters that you are evenly yoked in your belief system, yet a person's character, is highly underrated in comparison! Religious people get divorced too or stay unhappily married all the time, due to their commitment to God, yet your character is who you decide to be when nobody is looking, no matter what you profess to believe.

How could she make it? She was beautiful. On the scale of 1-10 most men I talked to over the 35 years gave her 8 to 9 on the scale of physical beauty. I had the pictures from her youth. I didn't know at the time; my experience and informal studies would lead me to write a book!

IN SEARCH OF A GOOD *CHRISTIAN* MAN

Did she know what to look for in a man? Did she have the tools? No, she didn't! All she had was guidance from older women, some who had a man, some who had a male, yet they all were "Christians" in her mind. I don't have anything against Christianity or Islam, yet what I learned in my life is this, "Character supersedes religion!" Whoever you are, is who you DECIDE to be. It doesn't matter what church or religion you profess to follow. I've seen it all, and every religion or denomination has its problems with some of the people that attend the services and represent them, from western religions to Islam. It's all about the people themselves. God is universal, and he works with imperfect individuals through spiritual principles and insight gained through nature and human experiences over millions of years! You see, that is another trap for you, thinking because the guy you are investigating is "in the Church," or he is a Muslim at a Mosque, that he is a good match. As I write this book, I'm reminded of a most recent incident where a pastor of a church was caught on video giving oral sex to a much younger sista who wasn't his wife. How about that for the one praying for your sins? Do not put your trust in the son of earthly men, I hear you. Social media was on fire with this video, and I'm sure his wife saw it or heard of it within a couple of hours or days. The next Sunday, he had a greatly reduced turnout at his church. I was shocked that he still had people in his church to support him. His response: "My weakness is BEATIFUL women." This is the guy you look up to in leading the flock. I'm not saying all pastors are like that. He is still of the "male species" and isn't perfect by any stretch of your imagination! What I am saying is again, "Character supersedes religion," in my humble experience. This book will help you determine the **character** of a potential mate because that is like a fingerprint, everybody has one, but they are all *different* under the microscope! Everyone is unique in character, and it stays with you for life! Any guy's character that you are thinking of dating is basically fully developed by age 25. In layman's terms sistas…if you are young or older and want to date a guy under 25 years old; then you need to determine the makeup of the "figurative bed", that he is sleeping on, before you date him!

We watch so many families go through many ordeals. By the time you are of dating age, you have subconsciously learned the ins and outs of pain displayed through anger, violence, depression, promiscuity, narcissism, drug and alcohol abuse, and triggered by uncalculated words spoken with the wrong tone or facial expression in imbalanced relationships between men and women, etc. I have also seen the beautiful relationships we have in our Black communities and why they work! As I write this book, I am in my mid-40s, divorced for over 20 years without children. I got married noticeably young. I had never lived with a female before. I had not figured out my own dysfunctional triggers at that time and how to overcome them. My childhood past came back to haunt me. The things I learned through experience. I thought that was the way to go, getting married young that is! Getting married young as a woman is key, yet that does not hold true for most men though, because a young Black man must develop other skills in the world to be able to take care of a wife, teach and help raise children, and to determine what type of woman he needs in his life, in a racist driven America! After the initial physical beauty and excitement wears off in his mind, through dating, in which all guys experience as young males; he will realize what else he needs in a long-term relationship as he decides to become a man or not! If you think about the alarming rate of single-parent homes without a father present in the Black communities, how is it even possible for a young man to choose a woman in this Modern society without him dating a few different types of females and women? A young man needs mentorship from an older man to help him figure out what is required of a man. Few males can accomplish this by the age of 25 in this Modern society without strong father figure lead mentorship! Personally, I must agree with the late GREAT Dr. Francis Cress Welsing when she stated that she thought Black women shouldn't have children until they were 30 years old and

Black men until they were 35 years old. She didn't say you shouldn't get married sooner, though! The key point to remember is that you as a female have a shelf life, regarding reproduction! I know you don't like to hear that but if you are considering having children one day, you should not waste your young years developing a "body count" in meaningless sexual relationships with random guys who don't care anything about you beyond sex! I'm sure Dr. Welsing was speaking of the Modern society after the 1980's crack cocaine epidemic and of our people with the invention of social media and fast-food dating! During the Baby Boomer days, you could totally see why they dated and married earlier. Unfortunately for the newer generation Millennials and Generation Z's after them, they are not as mature at an earlier age! Under ideal circumstances with balanced mature parents, I totally support sistas marrying in their 20's who have been taught to be good housewives. Social Media is the great time waster of our sistas! It gives you the illusion you have time after 25 years to 30 years old to "pick" a mate! The older you get, you become less desirable in the dating pool by guys for marriage. Your risks go up for birth defects as your eggs age. You also run the risk of pregnancy out of wedlock if you are having sex! These are just facts! I understand that looking back on my past and seeing the damage in the wake of dysfunctional and broken homes. I would like to have children also. At this point in my life, I want to write this book to help somebody else's family, since I couldn't help my own family growing up. I'm not the eldest sibling in my family. The older ones wouldn't dare follow me if it weren't but for pride alone. I made some serious sacrifices of my TIME trying to help my family improve their relationships in my youth. I spent the time trying to figure out myself and NOT to repeat the things that I witnessed in my family from my father. After I went through my divorce as a young man, I vowed not to marry again until I figured all this stuff out to protect my future legacy. Here I am, 25+ years older, with serious personal development and confidence in my truth. I'm writing this book to save someone the heartache I felt growing up from my young childhood to adulthood. I've learned so much in the past 3 decades! It's impossible to be a perfect man, yet I've strived to do the best job possible, at being a good man. After I figured out these key principles, which took all these years, I attempted to help my adult female friends, some listened, and some didn't! That is their choice. To this date, I've never been wrong about a guy that I analyzed for other female friends or associates and women that I met in my journeys in business. Now I'm focused on trying to help save the *next* generation if I can. Perhaps I can help some, while I figure out all I can about parenting as an older man. This was part of my story and a bigger part of my mama's life of which she never recovered from emotionally, in my opinion. I don't want to see you make the same mistakes as she did in choosing an effective life partner! I truly hope that you can learn how to make your "bed" better in your future! The last question I want to leave you with about my story is illustrated perfectly below. If you are already engaging in intimacy with the opposite sex, can you "honestly" say that you KNOW the makeup of his bed? You better do your due diligence sista, your future well-being is at stake! He might be a "sleeper cell" for you, like many I have met across this corrupt nation.

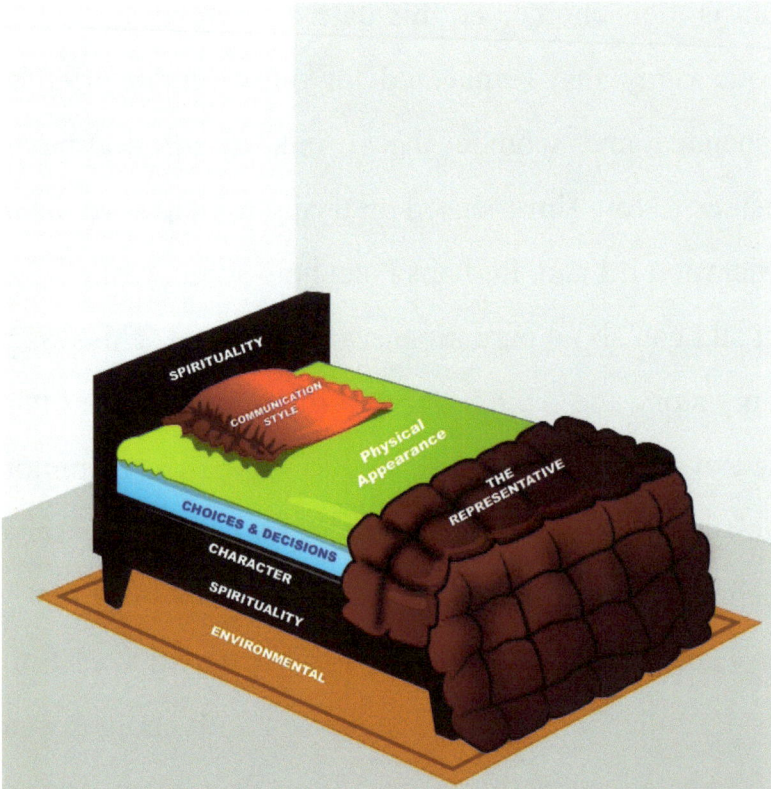

DO YOU REALLY KNOW
WHO IS SLEEPING IN "YOUR" BED?

Chapter 3:

THE GLOBAL AGENDA

It's time we stop telling each other lies and "feel-good stories" about how things should be in our minds. It's time to tell the REAL TRUTH! I'm going to help you gain valuable insight into how males view you and how men view you. We must stop buying into the global plan for us. The most powerful racists of the U.S. slave culture have a plan, and they have implemented it well worldwide and are still promoting it to the point that the next generation will not do well without serious guidance. I have traveled to several countries outside of America, and it is apparently clear to me. If we don't change what we view as good Black relationships now, there will be no need for bad press, entertainment, and education. Some Black authority figures and authors have drunk the Kool-Aid, so to speak. They believe that we are to blame for all that has happened to us, yet I consider them ignorant and not well

versed in socio-economic warfare and behavioral science.
"All Men are Males, but all Males are not MEN!" We
must determine who we allow to educate us. The same
goes for **females vs. women**. **Malcolm X** said it best.
"Only a FOOL let's his enemy educate his children!"

CHAPTER 4:

BLACK MEN AMONG US

I'm here for the sistas who still believe in Black Men and want to honestly know how to identify one. There is still a good shot that you can find a good Black Man with my help! This book is focused on the single sistas that did not have a good father figure to teach them how to identify a good Man when they engage the Black male population. There are also good fathers who didn't know how to teach their daughters to Pre-qualify a man beyond a few "old-fashioned" ideas like, make sure he has a good job, hardworking, God-fearing, honest and trustworthy. Yeah, that's great, dad, but what does that look like in real-time in the "21st Century" overwhelmed with Social Media dating and ideology? How can I tell if he is lying to me about core values and principles? How can I tell if he will be a good father if I have children with this dude? How can I tell if he is of good character and will not beat me up when he had a bad day at work or if I say something that he doesn't like, even showing him proper respect? How can I make it "unlikely" that he will have sex with other females, if possible? These are all the things to consider before you get your heart strings pulled.

In my opinion, the American Black Man, South African Black Man, and Haitian Man are the strongest Black revolutionary Men in the world because they are all fighters against the oppression that they have received from the Western cultural influences. The 21st Century Black man when you find him, is special beyond words! How fortunate you are if you find one, that is single and *emotionally* available and interested in being in a committed relationship with you, whether in marriage or a domestic partnership. You 2 must decide, nobody else can do so! Not to take anything away from my other Black and Brown brothers around the world; just know this, there is no other MEN as a group, on the face of the earth, who have fought harder under conditions of slavery, Jim Crow laws, and abuse in the last 500 years! And still, to this day, he is fighting for the right to get his respect in a world that doesn't love him back! Other brothers worldwide, at least, still have their *history, language* and know their *lineage* and *culture*. The American Black Man has lost all of that. When you, my sista, encounter an average to strong Black Man, you indeed have found someone GREAT! SHOW PROPER RESPECT FOR HIM. He has *survived* this system and still maintained his identity as a PRO Black community member on his journey to uplift our people by his example. We are public enemy number 1 because of what we stand for and how many of our forefathers have fought in World Wars and have fought in the U.S. and died...to give us a right to live as FREE MEN and WOMEN. Now we need to take the mental chains of slavery off. We need the help of our sistas! This is where good sistas come in. You are the key to birthing and assisting in raising and nurturing the next generation to *rebalance* the economic, cultural, and social scales of our Black communities across the world!

Men fight for the attention, affection, and protection of you in almost anything they do. I can break down the life from the cradle to the grave of our struggle in this system. If he didn't have the warmth of your touch, affection, and womb to protect our legacy, men would not be fighting so much for anything other than respect in a society that doesn't view us in a positive light. What would life look like if you knew how to choose a mate? Let me show you how. You think there aren't many Black men who want sistas as mates? Soon that might be true in most Western countries! It doesn't have to be your reality, though. There is a lot riding on both of us, but that argument is not relevant on this topic that there are not enough good Black Men to go around. There aren't enough good Black men to go around in America if you're looking *mainly* at over 6ft height, the financial status of 6 figures+, runway model, handsome, with a super muscular body and great in bed....oh and you are not on that same level yourself as his companion! There is PLENTY of GOOD BLACK MEN to go around for humble, respectful, nurturing, *feminine* sistas (not feminists) to join them. Every Black woman will not get a MAN, nor does every female DESERVE one... and vice-versa due to the dysfunctional family creating systems in place. We must further advance our people, and that is only going to happen with the right *couples procreating* to bring forth well-balanced children to join the ranks of a future solid Black Community.

I have learned the key questions to get answers that you can use to really *narrow* down your <u>*chances*</u> of dating and marrying a REAL BLACK MAN from the 10% chance you have now without understanding men. I will give you a 90% chance by following this checklist laid out later in this book. Based on where most of the sistas I've interviewed are over the years, if you have the discipline and humility to follow, you will win big!

The questions that you must ask your prospective Black guys in the beginning...will give you an edge over any other females! You see, my sista, I know EVERY type of guy there is in the Black Community. You must know what is beneficial to creating and sustaining long-term relationships.

You will have about a 90% chance of dating and marrying men over males (90/10 rule) with my checklist; in my opinion, backed by experience, IF you show DISCIPLINE...you can win in the dating game! Without this checklist, your odds are extremely low if you are looking for someone over 25 years old to date *seriously,* and you are below to an average-looking sista in face, body, and personality at best, in my experience wanting a man of good to great financial status! I don't care what age you are under 50yrs old! Social Media has made it cool to be lazy daters. Females are *ghosting* dates left and right. Wasting TIME...to get *older* and then become un-attractive for marriage by _society's standards_ due to too many *random hookups* with emotionally *unavailable* Black/Brown guys who are not interested in you past a sexual conquest or situation-ship in most cases. Some sistas end up giving birth to children who will be _fatherless_ in the _most important and delicate cycle_ of their lives due to poor choices and or preparation!

I am a Black Community activist, and I'm only concerned with rebuilding healthy Black families, not building more dysfunctional ones! We have enough of those already! If you are just looking to date endless random dudes, hey, this is not my focus, and perhaps you should keep looking for another feel-good book for that. Let my sacrifice of time be your gain. I already know there will be some critics of my experience and what I know about these issues. Please do comment and tell us of your vast knowledge. (smirk) This information is for those who are "humble" enough to accept instruction because you don't have much time!

You see, every man looking to start a family and grow his legacy isn't looking to *seriously* date just any Black/Brown sista. I want to protect "feminine" sistas who believe in and still love a Black Man *__leading__* the family. I will show you how to find out what type of guy you should be considering.

CHAPTER 5:

SO MUCH INFORMATION...YET UNFAVORABLE RESULTS

"WILL YOU SPEND YOUR 'BEST YEARS' IN THE WRONG DATING POOL?"

[Illustration] "Dating is like fishing; you must know what kind of fish swim in the waters(environment)that you are choosing to fish! The odds of getting a good man will

greatly be determined by your understanding of the 2 kinds of fish (males vs. men) that you will encounter and the "quality" of the fish that dominate in each dating pool!"

I have interviewed many sistas around the country, and I also have long-term friends that I have cared for throughout the years, and yet these sistas keep making the same mistakes looking for love in all the wrong places! They are some of the same ones telling me how much they *know* about this or that with men. Nah....Sis, if you really knew so much about us, why do you keep falling for or *failing* in the dating and relationship game to the point of marriage in some cases? They lack humility and are too stubborn to take guidance from the very one who has called all their relationship woes with 100% accuracy once I learned just a little bit about their love interests and or prospective mates, and I advised them with love. Yet, I know the journey. LOVE is blind, right? Western culture has taught our Black women that they can do whatever they want in relationships with Black guys without real consequences besides unwanted pregnancy. I'm sorry to break the bad news to you sis. You will ruin your life as a marriage mate option for most men. This isn't a dating book for several reasons. I do not believe that real MEN and WOMEN who are mature enough and contemplating commitment in a long-term relationship need *New Age* dating guidance! They are fully capable of communicating their needs upfront prior to a formal union like marriage!

They do need to agree on 6 things in my experience.

1: Spirituality – Are we going to support a religion or the universal laws that God put in place without going to a place of worship? Do we believe in an Almighty God, Technology, Science, or etc.?

2: Leadership – Will you follow your husband's decisions even when you disagree with him, if it isn't harming you or the children physically or emotionally? He shouldn't get lazy on taking care of his responsibilities to his wife and children either. He must maintain his presence as a loving father and supporter. Feminine women expect a guy to lead the family. Don't drop the ball bro!

3: Lifestyle -   Do we need a big house, expensive cars and or luxurious lifestyle to feel accomplished or content?

Do we feel the need to work toward financial freedom? Retirement? College fund for any children?

4: Communication – If we have an issue with each other, we shouldn't go to bed angry! That's the beginning stages of a future "side piece" or divorce! Let's discuss our issues honestly and completely to continue a balanced union of support and stability since you're considering marriage or a domestic partnership!

5: Respect - Even if we are upset with each other, we will not be disrespectful to one another. Don't let yourself go physically and expect your man's eyes not to wonder and get caught up elsewhere! This is disrespectful to guys who are already polygamist in nature! Be attentive to your woman's needs emotionally and physically also my brother, when she is doing her part.

6: Interdependence – You are depending on one another to do what you agreed upon as a unit before marriage drawing on the knowledge, you should have of each other in the dating phase. How you acquire a man is how you need to keep him. If you are sexy, fit and cooperative before you move in with him or marry him, then you need to keep that up! Guys with options are not so forgiving no matter what you say! Guys shouldn't make his woman work harder, if she is working fulltime, as well as taking care of the house and children while he is gone to work. He needs to assist her in whatever he knows how to do in the home. Don't be expecting dinner to be ready daily at a certain time when she also is working fulltime, and she isn't home in enough time to do so. He needs balance in his judgement and realistic in his expectations of his woman. You know the kind of woman you have at this point.

We must work together, and we won't act like we don't matter to each other, no matter what happens in this life!

Couples can figure the rest out if they are *honest* and *true* to themselves and their *potential* long-term partner. Would you, as a sista in your 30s - 40s, consider dating an 18-year-old male? You would probably say HELL NO! What if that 18-year-old was tall, dark, and handsome? What if he had a deep voice and muscular tone? Would you give him the cookies? Some would try to tell us that they would not, but I know he would get a few of you to give him some sweets at the very least...on the low! Most of you would say it is beneath you to even consider a boy as your MAN, right? Absolutely, you would say that, and rightly so. So here is the real question, why would you consider having unprotected sex with and OR seriously dating a grown male with an 18-year-old mindset??? Do you like to gamble at the casino? Doesn't the house win 99% of the time? Yet you still go back. Maybe you should also treat your relationships with males like that when you know the odds are against your relationship really working. Please don't get angry about it after you lose again and again with this mindset. Do we go to the manager of the casino and try to ruin it because we lost our money? Don't ask God for help when you take these kinds of chances to try to get a man out of the wrong dating pool for long-term commitments. You need to give your God something to work with. I am so serious. You see this every day! Steve Harvey wrote a dating book called "Think Like A Man and Act Like a Woman." Well, you can't do that if your dude isn't a MAN at all, thus the birth of this book, "The Checklist," and my pending book, "The

Blueprint." I'm not going to try to tell you who to date, ultimately you can date all the males you can handle! What I am going to instruct you on is the consequences of choosing the wrong kind of guy for what you feel could be or would be a long-term commitment with children in mind or view. My goal is to give you a head start in the dating pool or catch you up and align you with a successful strategy if you really want to date MEN as opposed to "just" Males. There are effectively 2 Dating Pools in life. {See Illustration} The 1st dating pool you are figuratively fishing in is a 90% Male Fish pool, and the 2nd Dating pool is a 90% MEN Fish pool. (The older standard was 80/20 rule, until Gen X had children and social media was born) They are CLOSELY related to each other. Few beyond your house of worship and your upbringing with a strong father figure can teach you how to fish for the highest quality that you personally qualify for when you don't know what is important to men! This is because, "figuratively" speaking, there is a little "tunnel of experience", that the fish go through between the pools, which is why some get into other pools! As the fish mature, they develop an appetite for certain types of food or types of females/women. You can find what you need or like in both pools, but the PROBABILITY is much lower depending on which "figurative bait" (dress, speech, attitude) you are using based on your personality, aligned with your true sexual market value as a female/woman, and the pool of which you prefer to fish! Some women have even told me that they would never take advice from a Man on the subject, of how to choose a guy! I silently am sad for them. Some of the same sistas go online being very passive-aggressive and speaking on their loneliness, not finding a good man, and they are well past 35 years old. Go figure. I can't tell them that it is likely over for them, if the men that they like, don't like or find them appealing enough for a commitment, and they will probably not be getting married and having planned childbirth like they expressed they wanted. Sistas can spend their whole life fishing in the wrong dating pool and once she reaches the downturn years beyond 45years+, when most of your "best" dating options are behind her, she is sometimes very pessimistic toward guys, due to her poor decisions in the past! If you were not taught, I understand, so let's make the best of your dating years now, shall we?

There are some very good-hearted and intelligent sistas, but in my research over the past three decades, I can tell you with _supreme_ confidence that most sistas who are intelligent and attractive _still_ fall to the seduction of males posing as MEN when they are young because of hidden insecurities within themselves, or because they want to _believe_ in them, due to the time and money, they have invested in him or having his children! Women tend to see what they want to see and ignore the facts. Unfortunately for you, my sista, time is not on your side, if you want to get married and have children for one man. This is yet another reason I blow off the few that will want to see all this data and statistics for my beliefs. It just shows that you are in denial, and nobody will be able to help you much anyways. Ask yourself, did that mindset serve you in the past few relationships you had with guys? You see, my view is based on firsthand wisdom on my group and countless interactions and experience with sistas over the last 35 years nationwide. What you need is honesty with yourselves and the ability to show discipline in your selection of prospects in the dating processes going forward with a systematic approach. If that isn't enough, just go to blackdemographics.com and the U.S. Census Bureau and gain some more insight into our dilemma as a people in this country. If you are in another country see your local national statistics for your group if you feel so inclined. You can go to The Pew Research Center online as well. There is evidence all around you!

Listen to me very carefully my dear. It will hurt a guy more in the wallet if his relationship fails. It will hurt everything in your life as a woman, if you fail to make a good choice in a mate when you are the one that will carry any children with a diminishing sexual marketing value to guys with options. If you reach 30 years old without good prospective marriage mates, honey, it is very likely you will reach 40 years old without a husband if you are not considered feminine, cooperative, beautiful in face, body, and personality. It may be worse if you have children already. There is no coming back most of the time in my experience. Guys are drawn to younger women all over the world. It is what it is. Yeah, you might know the comeback kid; hell, you might be the comeback kid, but those are EXCEPTIONS...not the rule! The truth can't be denied.

I will improve your ratio of dating MEN compared to just MALES if you are willing to demonstrate discipline, humility, and honesty...just let me lead you! I can't stress that enough because social media and dating apps tell you differently in your subconscious mind backed by social proofing through other females who profess to have it like that! Don't judge your success with guys by how many texts, video chats, dates, engagement offers, or how much money you or he makes. Judge your success by how many MEN you want to really be with, want to MARRY you, not how many male options you have! Yes, there is a difference, and if you don't know the distinct differences between men and males, you will lose most of the time! You see, the current western slave culture, with its great technology, has created way more males than men within its system. You don't think so? I ask you this question. "How many sistas do you know that have been with the same guy for 25yrs+ and they are at least 40 – 45 years old at this time, and they are still in a "happy" union? Can you think of at least 5 good sistas that YOU PERSONALLY have a relationship with where you live now (living grandparents included) who are in good relationships with a PRO "Black" Man who is well respected by other men as well? That experience and time frame would put them in the 1965s to 1970s baby category (40's – 50's age) Generation X or how about the Baby Boomers (65yrs old+ grandparents), which is earlier! If you say yes, put this book down and go get your advice from them. You might be alright. If you don't know 5 sistas in that space where you live, you need to cut off everything (Social Media) and focus on this book's guidance and study its content until you really get it! I believe that is the last eras where most of the Black Community members *knew* who their fathers and mothers were in America and had some level of positive participation in their upbringing. If not, we had real grandparents to take up the slack! Just look at the good Black content on the TV back then. We had The Cosby Show, A Different World, What's Happening Now, The Jeffersons, and Good Times to name a few. Contrast that with the entertainment we see on TV today. Housewives of Hollywood, Bridezilla, Wife Swap, Reality TV, and THOT (That Ho Over There) central are all over

Instagram! Can you see the differences? Nowadays, many youths have grown up without much assistance from their fathers due to prison, death, alcohol abuse, drug addiction, or deadbeat dad syndrome (just males) or raised by single masculine females who ran good men off! You see, GOOD BLACK MEN are around, yet they are not all the most handsome and financially well off as you might want them to be at the time, yet you can find some if you have a trained eye, and I will explain it all in my future book (The Blueprint). This is the Checklist. I have 2 questions that I will ask you in my upcoming book that you can contact me on my website, to answer these questions after you purchased and read this book. See my contact information at the end of this book. Subject line when you contact me is: Male vs. Man

**Question 1: * Is there a difference between a Male and a Man to you? (If your answer is NO, stop here)

***Question 2: What is the difference between a Male and a Man? (Do elaborate, this is not a trick question!)

Talk to me in your own words, so I know you are thinking for yourself and not cut and paste from the internet. Be specific as you can be. Don't give me just generic answers unless you really believe it is that simple for both questions.

I will likely give you a discount on the purchase of my future book called "The Blueprint" because I'm looking to protect high-quality sistas for healthy long-term relationships with Black Men. Your response will determine how I receive you. Respectable responses will gain positive and respectable results! I will be giving a discount code for those in Black and Brown nations due to the power of the U.S. currency in comparison to theirs. You will need to video chat (Facebook or Instagram) with me first, though, to make sure you are a person of African descent.

When you contact me, please let me know what part of the world you are from and are living in currently and give me your honest opinion of how you view yourself, on the sexual marketplace scale I put together. (Cooperation, Femininity, Nurturing Ability/Physical Appearance = 100% *total*) [*A* Guys viewpoint]

SEE the "Scales" portion of this book for details.

If you can't definitively answer these 2 questions, how can you go through life trying to find or date a man? You really can't. It's like rolling the dice and closing your eyes. How lucky are you?

You need to decide now. Is this book worth your time? However young or old you are, relationships cost you time and money that in the beginning is not calculated accurately, especially when your youth, innocence, children, and mental health are involved.

Divorces are expensive, and the price of your future children and or current kids has a value of way more than the cost of this book. You choose. Only the sista who is willing to take direction from somebody who knows the opposite sex well, will survive "emotionally" in the 21st Century dating Black Males vs. Black Men! You must be OPEN enough to receive new direction and disciplined enough to follow through on my advice to you, and I will promise you that you will find and date more men vs. males that you have been entertaining so far. This is a "checklist" for traditional women and Modern Day sistas who want to be housewives or domestic partners and who want to be loved and cherished by ONE man for the long-term, if not a lifetime. This book is mainly for the young sistas from 14 – 35 years old, although a single sista of any dating age who didn't have the guidance of a strong father figure for whatever reason can benefit greatly from its content. This book is intended for the younger single-parent mothers who don't have the proper information and want to be with a man. It's not all your fault if you have been misguided by older females who are scorned and disgruntled by their own bad choices in guys. Let me help you get out of the wrong dating pool or sustain you in the good graces of your existing man! Meanwhile, most of your peers or mentors are fishing in, the Male pool expecting stellar results! You can ruin your potential future with the best possible mate in your life from high school to college years mistakes, on ignorance alone! This is some of the most important guidance that you can possibly get from any one source.

Chapter 6:

The Checklist: Questions

Ages: 14-19 years

The High School Trap!

Before You Date!

Get to Know Your "Prospective" Friend or Boyfriend!

***Special Note**: If a boy is sagging his pants (underwear/boxers 'showing') ...don't even give him a chance! He is suffering from an identity crisis, and you can't help him! That "dress code" started in prison and stems from homosexuals letting others know they are available for sex. REAL MEN don't dress like that even in prison!*

Key Term Classifications for entire checklist:

Guys/Gals/Chics: Covers males and females, men and women in un-determined status, so it's a general classification; 18yrs+

Boys/Girls: Minors under 18 years old; adolescents

Males/Females: Selfish, immature young to grown adults

Men and Women: Responsible, calculated, disciplined; mature adults.

Get These Questions Answered "BEFORE" You Make Contact Outside of School!

1: What is your full "legal" name?

2: How old are you?

3: Where do you live, including the exact address?

4: Where did you grow up? city/state, street, neighborhood (6yrs – 14yrs)

5: Do you have a good relationship with your father?

6: Do you have a good relationship with your mother?

7: Were you adopted?

8: Who are your best friends?

9: What do you want to be when you grow up?

10: Do you plan on going to college/trade school/military?

11: Have you ever gotten anyone pregnant?

12: Do you have any children?

13: What are your top three favorite music genres (types)?

14: What do you like to do for fun?

15: Are you a virgin? If, no. Have you had any STD tests done, including HIV/AIDS tests? If yes, how long ago?

16: Do you have any drug or alcohol addictions? If no, have you tried any vices, like drugs—weed, cocaine, heroin, meth, etc.?

17: What do you want from this relationship?

Friendship? BF/GF? There is NO SEX, PERIOD!

Chapter 7:

The Checklist: Answers

Ages 14–19 years

The High School Trap!

Before You Date!

Get to Know Your "Prospective" Friend or Boyfriend!

1: You need to find out if this guy is who he says he is. He should have a student ID with his name and picture of himself on it or a government-issued Driver's License or Identification Card with his *current* address on it. We have too many young dudes lying to get over on young, naive girls in high school. If he doesn't have this, then he is in no position to befriend or date any young lady. Take a picture of it and let your parent(s) know where this boy who is interested in you for whatever reason lives.

2: Verify if his age matches his ID, do the math. If he is trying to be something that he is not, it is a red flag that he has bad intentions towards you and others. If he lies about his age, leave him alone, PERIOD!

3: If he doesn't have a government ID, then you need to know where this boy lives in case something happens to you while you are spending time with him. Your family needs to know where they can find him if need be. Verify his living arrangements at all costs if you are going to be with him outside of the school campus!

4: You need to know if he transferred from another area to see where he comes from and what his earlier environment was like. If he is from another place or another state, if you know where he grew up, you can determine some of what he is like and how it has shaped his thinking.

5: A boy's father figure is the single most influential personality in his life. If the boy doesn't know his father or he has set a bad example, this will prove to be a big issue for you, provided he doesn't have a surrogate or stand-in stepdad or grandpa to fill in the gaps for his **rites**

of passage. You don't want a guy who doesn't know what it is to be responsible. Meet his father figure if you can.

6: A boy's mother is the first person he loves out of the womb. A mom's job is mainly to shape his compassion and love for other people. If his mother is rough and not nurturing to him as a kid, he will not be able to love you properly if he doesn't have a surrogate woman to fill that void in his life. Ensure you find out who his mother is or his stepmom and how he honestly views this person. Hyper-Masculine females tend to raise effeminate boys or angry young emotionally charged boys.

7: If a boy was adopted and doesn't fully accept his foster parents as his own, emotionally, this will be a major weight on your shoulders to give him the nurturing that he still feels he didn't receive from them. You are not mature enough to be his mother, nor should you try to be! A sense of abandonment from his birth parents, especially his biological mom, will be a problem for you long-term. I believe this is too great a task to undertake at this stage. He needs to get professional therapy that you can't give him. I hope he is worth it, if you continue with him. Look at the movie Antwone Fisher by Denzel Washington. This will give you some insight. His stepparents need to be fully invested in his mental health and emotionally balanced themselves, for this young man to have a good start.

8: You need to meet his best friends and observe them closely. You need to know who your prospective friend looks up to or is leading. A guy chooses his friends based on his personality, in who he is or aspires to be, if he is being led by another man. You are given a blood family with relatives, but you choose your friends! This will give you keen insight into his belief system or what is important to him.

9: If a guy has no ambition for his future, you can't give him a future with you either. A guy that doesn't know what he is interested in by the time he reaches high school age has not been exposed to enough positive things or has possibly had his self-esteem crushed at home by his parent(s). You should not have to waste your youth trying to motivate him to push forward in life. This will drain you in the long-term, and heaven forbid you have his children. How tough are you? You will find out through your life. I recommend not overstepping, just being school friends, no further benefits outside of the school grounds.

10: If this person is at least a junior or a senior, he better know something by now. If he doesn't have a clue what his goals are at this point besides being a rapper, artist, movie star, comedian, etc. you need to run! This is a big trap for sure! You can't take care of a family without some real marketable skills. If he doesn't have a major record deal pending, you likely will waste your time and money. Be careful if he has no clue what he wants to do in his future after high school with some lucrative goals and a plan to get there. Pass on him for now.

11: If a guy got someone pregnant and now doesn't have children, you need to know what happened? Did he pressure her to get an abortion? How do you feel about that? I would say that if you are not ready to be a parent, then it is irresponsible to have unprotected sex. If he didn't know that or didn't care, it shows his weak mindset as a young male, and he is likely going to be just another "breeder," of which we have plenty floating around already! He should be nothing but a platonic friend, never a boyfriend, or "friends with benefits" relationship! Don't get caught up!!!!!!!!!

12: If a guy in high school has children already, wow! Listen, don't waste your time until he leaves school if you think he is worth it. See if he is going to make something out of himself without the promise of you on his side and riding on your income to take care of him. Don't get too comfortable with him. He already got a mouth(s) to feed. Any guy with any children in high school is a red flag. Run!

13: If he doesn't like anything but gangster rap/trap music, it shows he hasn't had much exposure in his life outside the hood. This could also symbolize his closed-mindedness as a guy. This will become apparent in trying new things to help him grow. A young guy should show some broader depth in his music selection which signifies he is able to grow mentally and spiritually.

14: Now you will see where his mind is from his own mouth. If he just plays video games all day, I feel sorry for you if you pursue him past friendship at this stage in his life! If he likes sports (not just video games), this is good, because this gives him a chance to learn new things and explore outdoors. Take heed to his likes, and you will learn about other things he will never say upfront. Just listen and take mental notes. See if your personalities are going to be compatible in the long-term. Be careful of your "nerd" gamer types! Spending all day online gaming, how will he be with a young lady? You better think about that aspect also. If you are also a gamer, that might work for a time, but true men need many "real-life" experiences to gain balance and wisdom to lead a strong family!

15: This is very serious. Once a guy starts having sex, it's going to be hard for him to stop! He will push you constantly to force you to have sex with him. This is how date rape happens in some cases. You should know about his sexual experience because it will shape your relationship with him. He also needs a test if he has been sexually active because there is no cure for HIV/AIDS, and it will kill some people over time. You don't want to have children with this disease. Some of the other Sexually Transmitted Diseases (STD) can damage your internal reproductive organs when you are of age and ready to rear children of your own one day. This can derail your plans for a family of your own, thus limiting your future marital options!

16: This is very important! When a person is addicted to drugs or other vices on a regular basis, it shows anxiety from some bigger issues that he is hiding. What happens when he doesn't have his alcohol fix? Weed? Hard drugs? You must get to the bottom of this before you decide to be with him. He could have very bad habits formed that will endanger your life by associating with him too closely, especially being his friend or girlfriend.

Here is the big one! After you have gathered all the data above, you can gauge if this prospect is "*leaning*" towards being a REAL MAN one day or just another MALE looking to become a "breeder" or playa. Be disciplined and don't settle for trivial things. This can ruin your LIFE if you choose poorly.

This checklist was <u>systematically</u> *put together with the knowledge of males vs. men in over 35+ years of study! Don't take this lightly, because your life is really on the line BEFORE you KNOW fully...who YOU are and aspire* to be one day! You're getting a glimpse of what it takes to be a Black Man in this society now. ***Perhaps the guys you thought were "not good enough" for you, are better than you knew, considering the struggle they survived thus far, in degraded environments under pressure!*** This is a "sorting process" for you to **refine** your tastes in young men, to give you a better chance at happiness with the right guy!

Chapter 8:

You Are Grown In The Eyes of the Law!

College Level Naive

19–28 years old

Checklist Q/A

Don't Get Pregnant Before Marriage!

Here is your best chance to meet and marry your future husband! DON'T BLOW it on partying AFTER your FRESHMAN YEAR! If you don't go to college, you REALLY got to be extra careful not to get caught up!

Ask these questions over time and get the answers that you need BEFORE any intimacy happens!

Some of the questions are the same as the previous high school trap checklist, so I will give the answers right after the questions.

1: What is your full "legal" name? (Show ME government-issued ID. If in college, show me your student college ID as well)

Answer: **High school is over, so any guys you decide to date need to focus on their future with discipline! He should produce official identification with his current address and his real name without much hesitation, if he is seriously interested in you.**

2: What is your interest in me? (Straight face)

Answer: [Option 1] Him: "Just kicking it, etc." **If you are still a virgin, this is a HELL NO! If you are *sexually* experienced, you better know what you are asking for because he just told you his "intentions" directly. RESPECT him for that. EXPECT NOTHING more than friends with *benefits* at best.**

[Option 2] "I want to get to know you better," etc. **OK give him a chance to know you and see where it goes. If he passes these questions below with accuracy and integrity (no lying) and if YOU like him also, proceed to the "dating phase" with discretion and focus!**

3: Where do you live?

Answer: **His current address should be on a government-issued ID. Then ask him if it is correct. You should drive by there *without* him later if you are going to give him a shot! Drive by in the daytime and at nighttime. See his environment, but don't approach his home! Be a GHOST! Listen to the sounds and watch the "street flow" of his community space.**

4: Do you live with anyone? If so, who?

Answer: **He likely has a roommate in the dorms or is living off campus. You need to find out who he is sharing his quarters with since you might be visiting him there one day. Date rape through brute force and drugs happen in his home, in vehicles, at clubs and house parties! You need to know the escape routes out of his apartment or home and neighborhood! Always let your "responsible" girlfriends know where you will be going at night, just in case!**

5: Do you have access: keys/security door codes/open window policies, etc., to any other females dwelling besides your blood sister(s) or close "elder" blood relatives? Don't count cousin's home!

Answer: **Guys who are not serious with you or anyone else generally builds a list of females to have sex with on any given night if he can! A guy's hormones are raging at this stage in his life. If he is not the type to want a legit girlfriend at this point in his life; he will develop access to other female housing arrangements for sexual options.**

6: What are you studying in college and do you have a real job or legal business that pays real bills? How long have you been working, consistently?

Answer: **Does he have a degree program that will generate enough income to support a family in relative comfort? He should be passionate about his career or it must be a degree program that is in demand in the marketplace. Any guy that gets a "junk" degree will likely suffer after college in a fast-paced world full of** digital change! Be prepared to struggle with him if he lacks vision and or hustle!

(Not in college/vocational school then SKIP to the job questions)

7: How are your grades? *(SKIP if not in school)*

Answer: **If he is not working, he should have decent study time and good to great grades legitimately! If his family is paying for his education, he should be really showing appreciation through his studious time and good grades. If he isn't serious about his career and has student loans in the end, he will not be a good companion with college debt and no real craft. The best career jobs go to those with the best GPAs, backed by real focus and discipline!**

8: Do you have a good relationship with your father? If no, why?

Answer: **(SEE Previous Checklist)**

9: Do you have a good relationship with your mother? If no, why?

Answer: **(SEE Previous Checklist)**

10: Do you have any childhood traumas? Sexual abuse, physical abuse, drug abuse, verbal abuse?

Answer: **I don't recommend dating a guy that has been sexually or extremely physically abused up front, without at least 1 - 2 years of weekly counseling and therapy! He must give you access to his therapist and or counselor for some honest conversation of his "progress", granted that it was prior to meeting you! If he shows signs of suppressed trauma through violent emotions, outbursts or depression over small things, you need to keep looking! You are going to be out of your league; trying to support him beyond your capacity in most cases! What happens when we bring children into a mentally, physically and financially unstable environment? Another dysfunctional generation is born!**

11: Were you adopted?

Answer: **(SEE Previous Checklist)**

12: Where did you grow up?

Answer: **(SEE Previous Checklist)**

13: Who are your best friends?

Answer: **(SEE Previous Checklist)**

14: What are your top three favorite types of music genres?

Answer: **(SEE Previous Checklist)**

15: What is your favorite song and why?

Answer: **This will explain his current mindset on some core level. Take note!**

16: Have you ever been in love before? If so, how long ago? How long did the relationship last? Why did it end? Have you ever *had a side chic (not random sex partners)* while in a committed relationship? If so, why? *A **"side chic"** is a regular chic he is seeing, **not a random hookup**, he could have some *real* feelings for a side chic!

Answer: **A man's capacity to love starts with his mother. BASED on your previous data (refer to his relationship with his mother figure question above) you should be forming an opinion on his ability to properly love a woman at this point. Has this guy ever been in a long-term "loving" relationship? This data will help you to see if he has longevity and balance! If he only has dated the same girl/chic/woman for no more than 1year or less, then he doesn't promise much at this point. He doesn't know what he wants in a woman or he just loses interest fast, which means he is not ready for a serious relationship in most cases. Date more mature guys if you are "truly" a balanced young woman! Ask him what went wrong in the other relationships. Then ask him if he did anything wrong. What did he learn from the experience? He should** have something meaningful to say or you might be wasting your time if he is over 21 years old and not an introverted type. Then again maybe you need to run anyways! (laughing) Listen, if you are into socially awkward guys, just know you will likely have to lead your relationship in most things. Now let's talk about the "side-chic" thing. Having a side chic doesn't necessarily mean he didn't like or love her. Perhaps she was doing something his girlfriend was not willing to do at the time. She could have been giving him a different type of respect also. There are too many reasons to list here. You will have to ask him why he needed one in the past.

Some guys require different things physically and emotionally. They don't all just want a "side piece" for variety or show! Some females provide rare services hard to find in 1 woman so far in his dating experiences.

17: Have you ever hit, thrown, or choked a girl/woman before? If so, why?

Answer: **You want to know if he is "uncontrollably" violent. If he answers yes to any of the above mentioned, your next question should be, "Were you dating her or in a relationship with that person?" If yes, get the story of what led up to that and what he did to her. Did she push his buttons to the limit? Did she slap or hit him? Make your decision on what you are willing to endure or risk, after he is emotionally invested in you and you must make hard decisions after the fact!**

18: Have you ever gotten anyone pregnant before? If so, what happened?

Answer: **(SEE Previous Checklist)**

19: Do you have any children?

Answer: **He is a grown male/man now. He is not in high school anymore. You need to know if he has** children and is he spending time with them. If he isn't attempting to see his child(ren) then he is unfit to have a family with you! A real man will instinctively want to care for his seed. If the mother of the child doesn't give him a path to do so, then that is different, yet you need to investigate that story he gives you! The implications of a "deadbeat dad" need not continue in your life!

20: Do you have a bad temper? What pisses you off besides these questions? (smile) (Ask him to elaborate, non-aggressively)

Ask him to give you examples if need be.

Answer: **Keeping a grown "male" out of trouble is a fulltime job! Do you really want that headache considering the problems with police brutality and trivial conflicts in this society with entitled people everywhere calling the police? You judge for yourself based on his answers.**

21: Have you ever been arrested before? If so, for what? Do you have a juvenile record? If so, for what? Do you have a felony(s)? What did you do? Can you get any felony(s) expunged?

Answer: **It is commendable that this guy is trying to better himself. Be careful to monitor his style from a distance, to see if he has great discipline. He needs a "business degree" or skilled trade in some field where his police record won't be scrutinized heavily, so he can make real money after college! You need to know if he has issues you can cope with and understand, or not!**

22: Do you plan on ever having a family of your own through marriage, including child(ren)?

Answer: **Now is the time to get definitive answers before you waste precious childbearing years, if he is or isn't interested in having a wife and child(ren). Don't assume you know, ask!**

23: Do you have any drug or alcohol addictions currently? If no, have you *tried* anything **besides weed**, like cocaine, heroin, meth, etc., in the past? If yes, then why? How long ago? Did you stop?

Answer: **If a guy is an occasional or regular weed smoker and you are ok with that, then there is no issue! When a guy has a "vice," like the above-mentioned addictions, you need to keep it moving! I shouldn't have to tell you what that leads to. For example: brain damage, severe accidents, depression, mental illnesses, anxiety, violence, crime, and death!**

24: Have you had any mixed sexual feelings about other guys? Are you bi-sexual or bi-curious? Have you had any sexual experiences with other males? Answer: **By now any guy knows what his preference is sexually. Now you need to know your competition directly. Just ask him straight up, and just wait for his response, including watching his body language!**

25: Do you have a hard time expressing your emotions to a woman that you care about?

Answer: **Good communication is key to long-lasting balanced relationships. If he can't express himself well, can you handle that? I know plenty of women who got tired of talking and dragging information out of a guy because he was a poor communicator.**

26: Do you believe in a higher power? Almighty God, Allah, or others like aliens, etc.? Atheist (God doesn't exist)? Agnostic (not sure)?

Answer: **What dictates how a guy will treat you besides the law? The "God concept" has always kept a man balanced in his conscious moves since the beginning of time! If he doesn't believe he has to answer to a higher power, what makes you think he can honor you appropriately in a serious relationship? The Modern World has left the guidance of old, so if you get an atheist or agnostic believer, then how will you balance the union long-term? Ask social media for answers from other blind peers or snake oil salesmen?**

"Google" that! He needs to know something on the subject!

I'm a Single Parent in my 20s - 30s

"I've **never** been *married*, ***don't*** have any ***housewife skills*** and I'm ***average looking at best***, with ***below to average body***. What are my options for marriage to a highly successful man?"

Sista, let me be totally honest with you; you are "unstable" to the average or high value man in your age range. You will be used for friends with benefits relationships in ***most*** cases, although males won't tell you that and the strongest, most successful men, will simply not want to commit to *marriage* to you. You are not marriage material in most average men's eyes your own age and older. You will likely find better options with an *older* man at best. Hit the gym *hard* at the very least!

You might find a MAN if you are friendly, humble, fit, submissive and not high in maintenance. You must work on your physical body and your mindset towards cooperation with a Man. Every woman can do a lot to change her physical appearance without being "obsessively" fake-looking! You need to learn some *housewife* skills from other *great* wives.

Here is my math for the below-average to average-looking Sista or Latina. I would be doing you a disservice by making you believe otherwise like other women will tell you in your circle, to make you feel better! In a guy's mind *consciously*, he will think he can do better than you, and he will be looking to trade up! This is one reason he will be seeing other females on the side or trying to do so, if you get him to even commit with his words to be your man, not husband. You can expect to share him with other females whether you know it or not! If he is sustaining you, keep quiet, if you can't sustain yourself long-term, but make some adjustments in how you plan your future in case he leaves you one day for another woman. If he is good to your child(ren), then you must keep him happy at least until your children are grown because it is rare, to have a financially stable Black man that takes care of you and your average looking at best, with child(ren) in the household that are not his! You must *sacrifice* for your children at this point! It's better to be with a man that provides and protects your family, than to be with males who are liabilities, and please don't bring home males to your minor child(ren), ever! If guys that you want are not really into you, your challenges will be great while child(ren) are still growing daily! You can call this *sexist* or whatever you like. This is LIFE! It is what it is! There are *__always exceptions to every rule__*, but don't count on that *guiding* you because **TIME** isn't on your side! There is a good reason why there are *overwhelming* numbers of single parent sistas in the church with no man present. They are still waiting on God to send them one to *their* liking. Go up and ask them how long they have been waiting at the ripe age of 40yr old+. God don't work that way sis! I'm sorry you were told otherwise. Give it to the Almighty God/Allah and the Universe but do YOUR part too!

This is what I have seen throughout my 35+ years of observation and study. Take it or leave it; just don't fool yourself! Pay attention to my personal opinions backed by 35+years of *active* experience studying Black and Brown people on the low! I'm not trying to make you feel bad; I'm just giving you reality. The truth is I *LOVE* you, my sista! I would tell my daughter the same things if I had one.

Global Dating Is REAL

Look at how many young women there are in the world that are turning 18 – 21 years old daily! Now with the power of the internet, there are so many guys *online* trying to find a woman from other countries to bring to the Western world who is attractive, sexy, loyal, family-oriented, and willing to follow a man's lead in the family. I've seen this with my own 2 eyes! I've been on **4 continents** to this day and several countries and let me tell you, you have real competition, believe it or not! Sure, there are gold diggers in every country and bad relationship choices even abroad. This isn't stopping guys from going for it because, honestly, the odds are in their favor if they know what to look for in a mate! Yet it is still *easier* to find a Black/Brown woman here, without all that paperwork importing a partner/wife, etc. Black men and others are *actively* pursuing them in Eastern Europe, The Caribbean Islands, all-over Latin America, all-over Southeast Asia, and Sub-Saharan Africa!

You can win if you know how to carry yourself and know what MEN value!

I'm not asking you to compromise who you are, but if you are *disrespectful*, out of "decent" *physical shape*, and *masculine* you will lose in the long-term! Being below to average looking *isn't* an automatic failure, though. Just don't look for **highly** successful men making $100,000/year or more as your *standard*, he has so many **younger** and more **beautiful** options at that level! If you are not blessed with good looks or a great body, there is still plenty you can do to gain the affection of a real man, provided you have a balanced personality and willing to control your weight and physical fitness in the long-term. See the information *below* on how you can somewhat *compete* against younger and more *physically* attractive women.

SINGLE PARENT "DATING" ADVICE!

SMV (Sexual Market Value) On a scale of 1 - 10!

***Females are the gateway to sex, and guys are the gateway to relationships! Yeah, you have been taught wrong!

3 Things Black "females" want:

1: The authority of a man

2: The advantages of a woman

3: The accountability of a child

3 Things Black "women" want:

1: Protection of a Man

2: Unity that femininity creates

3: The rewards of marriage

"1" is the least attractive (*without makeup and implants*) female/woman. "10" is the finest sistas (*without makeup and implants*) walking the earth.

The concepts below are approximate ranges to give you an idea of what everyday guys prefer from my experience. Just don't take these scenarios for granted because of your **Americanized** ego! When you bring children into the world, you must live for them *until* you acquire a man, and if you can get a man that YOU want to marry you, great! You should consider yourself **very blessed**! There are *not many* "upper" middleclass Black Men to high-income earning and "select" Black Men who will want another man's child to raise these days! I'm just giving you the facts. If you can acquire one, don't mess this up by ridiculous social proofing of your peer group and social media influences! I am in no way trying to hurt your feelings on this subject because I do want you to win in the dating game. It wouldn't be the *norm if you gained middle class to high-income earning men to want to "marry" you at this point*! If you focus on men a bit older (40 years old+) will give you a better shot at finding a man who can support you emotionally and financially enough to raise *your* young children to adulthood when you are young yourself, and not a multiple 6-figure income earner!

"+" (See info below: equals your age and the "likely" number of the age of the prospective "MAN" that would be willing to date you _seriously with marriage in view,_ if YOU have the right attitude, personality, and humility and you are in good "physical" shape, based on _his_ preferences, not yours, etc.).

For Example: If you are 18 years old and below average like a 4 and have a child, you would be approximately looking at a +25. Meaning you would _likely_ have a better CHANCE at dating a mature man at 43 years old than another 18- to 35-year-old dude who doesn't know what a MAN really is in most cases today! Your baby is already here. They soak up any negative or positive energy you put in its life. You will find out how good or bad of a parent you were by the time your child reaches high school! It's too late by then. LISTEN to my words, my sista. This ride only goes one way, FORWARD in TIME, NOT backwards! Sacrifice or DIE alone! It was your choice to start having sex with this guy(s), and now you will suffer the consequences for making these mistakes, _unless_ you were raped. Men would make some allowances in that regard, but still most guys will want to pass on marriage to you, to be honest.

Some will disagree, I'm sure, yet real-life will teach you the truth, and I hope you accept it BEFORE you pass up your best choices in a good mate for yourself. This is considering you are in <u>good to excellent physical shape</u>!

1-7 females with a great and submissive attitude generally only get Average males or men to marry them at best, in most cases with child(ren) under 18 years old living in the home. I'm telling you what men have said in the inner circles and felt for years about seriously dating women of any race for marriage! You are in the inside of the minds of so many guys thoughts, that Western society dares them to say out loud!

1-7.5 Scale 18 – 25 years old w/ 1 a **respectful** child +25 man

1-9.5 Scale 18 – 25 years old w/ 2 **respectful** children + 25-35 minimum man

18 – 25 years old and up w/ 3+ **respectful** children or not won't get married in most cases! "You really don't want to be here, but you will get tired of raising boys

without a father, especially in the poorest places to live."

Fatherless boys get into all kinds of trouble, and fatherless girls bring home babies by other insufficient fathers. They are also vulnerable to be raped and sometimes killed by males from the streets. They are likely to grow up without healthy self-esteem if they survive their childhood. There are no MEN protecting them, so they are like baby Antelope on the African plains "lost" without the herd. Predators are everywhere, waiting to devour them!

Special Note: I must mention this because I hear this entirely too much! "I got all of these guys trying to get at me!" "I KNOW I got it going on." "They want these cookies honey; my body is perfect!" "I got cakes and ice cream in the same shop!" Oh really? Let's perform a test. Tell them you are not interested in having sex with him (Straight face) you just want to be platonic friends, if he doesn't try anything. You are saving yourself until you are married now. Tell him that you won't be getting in a car with him, and you are not going to meet him anywhere outside of a public place. (straight face) Sista, NEVER judge how good of a *catch* you are by how many guys want to have sex with you! There will *always* be *somebody* willing to hit it! Sex is like eating to a guy. He needs it twice a day or more, and the next day he has forgotten the taste of the meal and wants to eat again. Nothing qualifies you better than a man that YOU like and wants to MARRY you! Most males will say anything to get the cookies. You think that makes you special? It doesn't! I know many guys over the years who just want to get their numbers up to brag to other guys or to satisfy his manhood cravings. He doesn't have to like you or love you to hit it. Below average girls/women get it just the same. Stop using that as a *qualifying* mark for long-term relationships up to and including marriage. It is nothing to a guy over 25 years old who isn't a virgin and has had his fair share of sexual experiences already! It's just cookies and milk....no more and no less! After he is full (climaxed), he doesn't even know why he wanted "it" that bad!

A Little-Known Secret for 25year old+ and Seriously Dating A Guy

Do you want to know if you mean anything to a guy you are dating over a 1 year? Is he a quality prospect who you think can be the ONE? Just ask him about your relationship and where it is going after you "break him off" properly (if you are having sex already, if not…skip this part) and he has had his nap, his mind will be *clear as it will ever be,* and you will see what is in his heart because the thirst has been quenched! You decide what level you are at with him based on his demeanor and body language, then see if you are just a side-chic or just the main chic who he isn't really committed to while he waits on a better option for himself since you don't have it (longevity). A thirsty guy never speaks truth! Quench his thirst and look into his soul through his eyes. What he says or doesn't say speaks volumes on your relationship or situation-ship!

You always want to pursue a guy in your range! Don't try to date a 9-10 when you are a 5 without your makeup and natural hair. Remember, guys are not judged in this society by their looks as much as their status with power and income. I know it sounds superficial. Don't think I don't know how it sounds. Do you want to be just a booty call, or do you want your own husband? Here is the key to all of this. Guys mainly see things like this, although most of them are *not going to tell you to your face,* no matter how much pressure you put on him, if he cares about you enough and thinks you will stop giving him the cookies. Actions speak louder than words, though. ONLY men will tell you what you are doing wrong, not grown males. Males will lie until the end of time!

These are approximate (below), but you will get the picture. This is in *percentages* for descriptive purposes ONLY based on my 35 years+ experience, not from data from some research company online. Although one just needs to look at the celebrities that have the most power/money. Research shows most *confident, successful, and beautiful* women look for financial and physical security first, then everything else for long-term relationships. Just look at the numerous "*gold digger*" videos on YouTube/ Facebook, etc. The *thirst* is real! I know that isn't all women, just the most attractive ones. They have options, so can you to some degree, if you weren't blessed with natural beauty in face and hair, because you can do many things to improve your body without being fake!

Here are how the "most confident" guys choose their women for a long-term relationship unless they met them during their rise to success in *business* with their love...

and even then, some trade up to what they think they are personally worth. Take heed!

(Cooperation, Femininity, Nurturing Ability/Physical Appearance = 100% *total)* vs. His *likely* qualities

***Most people are average at best! You know the scale below applies to the average Modern-Day female because very attractive, feminine, respectful, and non-combative sistas without children don't have to read a book to get a high-quality man, if they know what real value is in a Man. They had a good example and upbringing, generally from a 2-parent traditional household or a mother figure who was balanced, which is rare these days in the Black community!

"THE SCALE"

You (Cooperation, Femininity, Nurturing Ability/Physical Appearance = 100% *total) vs. His Qualities.*

If you are attractive, fit, feminine, and humble, without children in the home, you will have no problem gaining a good husband if you are under 30 years old. As you get older without prospects, guys will begin to question why you are still on the market, no matter the reason you give. It's like a house on the market that was for sale over 3 months at a very high inflated price. Then 6 months go by, nobody bought it at that price, because the market has spoken! You can hold out at that price, or you can lower your price tag. Whether you agree with me or not, I must be honest with you about what men really think. We look at it like that and say to ourselves and others, why hasn't this woman gotten married? You might say it's because you didn't want to get married due to your career goals or not able to find the right guy. Well, either way, as time goes on, you are valued less on the market with single eligible men! You can date all the guys you want; that don't count to men. You say you can live with that, well, until you hit your down-market point, and nobody is seriously interested in you that YOU want, personally! I'm trying to save some sistas from a life of misery and prevent them from chasing bad boys and or wealthy men in their later years. Listen, we all have a marketable scale and price. As men get older, he gains value, assuming he grows his intelligence and income. Women, on the other hand, can't be judged by other women, unless you are marrying a woman. You must gain advice from an alternative source if you want the truth. Your single girlfriends can't give you that. That is like asking somebody in a sinking ship with you in the open ocean to save you, hell they can't save themselves! They are in the same boat sinking with time!

Some of you might be thinking, this guy is crazy, "I know so and so who got a good man, and he is only this age or that." You don't have any real statistics, etc. Blah Blah Blah. Listen, test it out and really open your eyes and see outside of your comfort zone and your sphere of influence amongst older failed females. Notice how many sistas are alone. Ask them what happened? Get the full story and remember as they tell their stories, is she leaving anything out, what did she do to disqualify herself at an early age? Look outside your support for another Black or Brown single (feminist) female or out of shape and combative one. Get the back story of the relationship, and you will see...4 things likely went wrong:

1: She was never taught how to be a Woman or wife by a responsible sista, and he found someone else who he felt did treat him with respect and cooperation.

2: She NEVER started with a MAN in the first place...which means she had just a MALE, yet she chose him.

3: You got lazy with how you treated the MAN, physically let herself go and stopped doing the things that you did in the beginning when you first met, or he determined that you were lacking some key qualities that he feels a wife should have or acquire.

4: You dated a man who never wanted to get married to you. Perhaps he didn't want to get married to any woman in the first place!

The other downfall in relationships like the above-mentioned is, sometimes sistas get pregnant and stay with him for that reason, which is NEVER a good idea if he isn't a MAN in the first place. But you should have thought about that before you had unprotected sex with him. How is having one or more children for him going to solve your issues with him? He could be wrong also, but we are not talking about him right now. This book is to help YOU get to the next level with favorable results because a guy can always find another good woman at any age of his life! If a male is over 30 years old, it's already highly unlikely for him to be a great MAN mentally, not financially. Life is short; some things must happen at an earlier age, called effective training. He still can become an average man one day, if he chooses to be, that is another book altogether!

I'm just here to tell you, if you or the girl you are thinking about is below average or average and her guy is, in fact, a MAN who has options...then she had better be humble, intelligent, and good to him, because he is rare, if indeed, he isn't seeking to trade up in a bad relationship! Even if a man loves the children, some will have sex with other women if she doesn't take care to keep herself up physically. The tradeoff sometimes happens later in the relationship, but it still happens. It's on his mind whether you know it or not. Guys judge women by how they take care of "themselves" and their view of class and the relationship with him. If you don't take care of how you look, it sends signals to him of *low self-esteem,* which will make him feel he is losing and can do better. A lady couple's therapist recently told me in her practice *men cheat to stay, and women cheat to leave*. I believe that is very accurate. I see married men having sexual affairs with other women to stay in the relationship and for their children to be in 1 home. You can't guarantee a guy won't have sex with other women. Yet you can do all you can to deter him naturally by how you take care of yourself and him. You need to know the kind of man you are dating or married. All that is out the window once they (children) go to college or leave home as young adults. This is something he can't constantly tell her if he loves her because it doesn't sound loving, but a guy is wired differently from you! He considers it disrespectful for you to let yourself go and think he will just stay with you no matter what. Some guys feel he is doing you a favor by even being with you. You just don't know how this plays out in your relationship over time until it is too late. I'm not here to give you false hope or stroke your ego. There are plenty of women groups to do that already. My goal is to get your mindset recalibrated to win the *competition.* Who _believes_ "the hype" that social media _promotes_ to Black and Brown women, that you have all the time in the world to find a good man? It is simply a trap, and you wake up much older _wondering_ why you have no *real love* in your life. You would have wasted your youth on some B.S. New Age ideology! I support women's empowerment, but this is not it! This is delusional Information Age bulls**t that will keep you single!

Chapter 9:

Single with Children

(35 years +)

Use the previous questions above to get you in the ballpark to find a good man. Here is what you need to know, though. Your options are greatly limited if you want a man without children who wants children of his own and he is not willing to adopt and or help you raise your existing minor children. You might have a shot if they are out of the home and if you are excellent in all other areas!

Don't waste your time trying to change him. You don't have the time to waste. Here is what you should be doing with every free moment. You should be working on your skills to add to a man's life! The "lost art" of how to be a housewife in the U.S. is gone, for the most part! You need to be learning how to be a better parent and working out, religiously! Be in the best shape that you can possibly be. Believe it or not, the better shape you are in, the better chances will be that you will attract a man willing to help you finish what you started on your journey with children. If you let yourself go physically, no matter how many jobs you have or whatever responsibilities you have with raising children, it doesn't matter to men. Men will not change no matter what you hear your single scorned and or dysfunctional girlfriends tell you! They will find a way to get what they want or die trying to achieve his hearts desires. That will involve having sex with multiple women along with you until he finds what he considers a good woman for marriage. That might not be you, so understand that you are still not married and have no covering!

You must keep it together, and you will get more REAL options than your other sistas who do not. This is your time to shine, don't waste your window being stubborn. Trust me, most women that reject the things I'm telling you don't likely have a man at home that is above average in any way! I want to see our Black communities rise again. It will take work on all our parts. You see there is a limited amount of emotionally, mentally, and physically available strong Black MEN in America of any age right now at the middle-class to higher income levels of $75,000 - $100,000+ and beyond! Do you notice that there are many Black Men with money and resources taking wives from other ethnic groups? What do they all have in common? They are feminine, supportive, submissive, and in decent to amazing shape. This matters more than you know. It's my goal to teach you how to win, and I will go into detail in my upcoming book. This "Checklist" is to help you stop wasting years dating MALES and not MEN while I finish "The Blueprint." Once you start down that path and you fall in lust or love with a MALE, you likely will see it through to your emotional destruction as most of my older single Black lady friends and others have done to this day! At the end of their youth, they are angry and alone, with half-grown to grown children with lower self-esteem. They become single in their 40s - 50s with very few options when they operate out of desperation or anger, neither qualities that men seek in a woman.

Everything applied must be done in the right *order* and with DISCIPLINE. I can teach you that. Hang on sistas. Help is on the way!

Chapter 10:

The Checklist Questions

Grown Women/No Children

(35 years +)

Special Note: Remember "The Scale"

1: What is your full "legal" name? (Show ME a government-issued ID) *Allow him to cover his address on the ID.* You don't want him to think you are a stalker! Tell him that also.

2: What is your interest in me? (Straight face)

[Option 1] Him: "Just kicking it, etc." He just told you his "intentions" directly. RESPECT him for that. EXPECT NOTHING more than friends with *benefits* at best. *He isn't really interested in you.* [Option 2]

"I want to get to know you better," etc. OK, give him a chance to know you and see where it goes. If he passes these questions below with accuracy and integrity (no lying) and *if YOU like him also*! Proceed to the next question.

3: What city do you live in?

4: Do you live with anyone? If so, who?

5: Do you have access/keys to any other females' dwelling besides your blood sister or blood relative?

6: What do you do for a living and for how long?

7: What is your 5-year plan?

8: Do you have a good relationship with your father?

If no, why?

9: Do you have a good relationship with your mother? If no, why?

10: Do you have any childhood traumas? Sexual abuse, physical abuse, drug abuse, verbal abuse?

11: Were you adopted?

12: Where did you grow up?

13: Who are your best friends?

14: What are your top three favorite types of music?

15: What is your favorite song and why?

16: Have you ever been in love before? If so, how long ago? How many times? How long did the relationship last on average? Why did it end?

17: Have you ever hit, thrown, choked a girl/woman before? If so, why?

18: Have you ever gotten anyone pregnant before, and they had it aborted? If so, why?

19: Do you have any children? If yes, do you spend time with all of them regularly? If no, why not?

20: Do you have a bad temper? What pisses you off besides these questions? (Make him elaborate)

Make sure he gives you examples if need be.

21: Have you ever been arrested before? If so, for what? Do you have a juvenile record? If so, for what? Do you have any felonies? What did you do?

22: Do you ever plan on having a family of your own?

23: Do you have any drug or alcohol addictions currently? If no, have you *tried* anything *besides* weed, like cocaine, heroin, meth, etc.?

24: Have you had any mixed sexual feelings about other guys? Are you bisexual or bi-curious? Have you had any sexual experiences with other males?

25: Do you have a hard time expressing your emotions to a woman that you care about?

26: Do you believe in a higher power? Almighty God, Allah, or others like aliens, Etc.?

Atheist (God doesn't exist)? Agnostic (not sure)?

CHAPTER 11:

GROWN WOMEN/NO CHILDREN

WHY ASK THESE QUESTIONS BRO?

(35 YEARS +)

I will now go into the reasoning behind such *simple* questions. You might be looking for some magical words, etc. Life is not like that. I feel for our women because society has given you so many options with these phones, social media, other apps, etc. You have not learned what makes relationships between men and women work! You are bombarded with so much information but little real-world education. Here are the reasons I asked these specific questions and the wisdom you will gain from asking these questions in these specific ways before you become emotionally attached to a male and not a MAN, on ignorance! You must MAINTAIN DISCIPLINE, or this will NOT work out well for you! You can NEVER beat a guy at being MASCULINE, and a guy can NEVER beat a chic at being FEMININE in the real-world sense! They are opposites and that is why masculine and feminine people work well together. When these opposites come together, they create real balance and harmony like they were intended. MEN will NEVER compromise their happiness forever if they feel they have better options, because he knows his time is short on this earth! He is mentally conditioned to battle to receive the best he can, while he is here on this earth! You must understand and know if you don't get on his program, he will find somebody else who will! It's in his NATURE to continue to HUNT, get all the resources he can qualify for until he either wins the game in his mind or DIES trying to WIN! Remember that going forward! Nothing you can say or do will stop him if you are slacking!

Special Note: These questions can be answered over the course of maybe **1 month** of **_daily_** communication and interaction if you are worried about running him off! Let me tell you this, if a man is REALLY into you, he will not be deterred by these questions! These questions are designed to be asked face to face or even over video chat if you must, but preferably in his face in a public setting!

A man that really wants something will be patient. If he is deterred, that should be a red flag to you. He is hiding something that he doesn't want you to know about him, but you should know. Don't skip these questions, and you make sure you don't give him any cookies and milk before you got all these questions answered favorably for your future well-being!

Listen up sis! Here we go. Are you ready? It's time for grown folks to talk!

Chapter 12:

The Checklist: Answers

Grown Women/No Children

(Why These Questions Bro?)

1: You can't research a guy if you don't even know his government name. Don't check him out until you finish all the questions. Allow a man to stand in his truth. By the end of the other questions, you might already be ready to toss him from your list anyways!

2:You must be serious here. If a man likes you, he will tell you straight up. [Option 1] If he just wants to hang out and kick it. That means sex, not a committed relationship; respect him for telling you the truth. That doesn't make him a bad guy, just not emotionally available to you. You really shouldn't gamble at this age. Most guys under 40 years old crave sex daily!

[Option 2] "I want to get to know you better," etc. OK, cool! Now ask him, "are you talking about just friends with benefits relationship or real dating that leads to a committed relationship in 2 months of no intimacy, with marriage being the ultimate goal?" Take your time and get these questions answered before you do anything sexual with him. If he pauses too long, he about to try to lie! If he doesn't answer that, he is trying to play you. Maintain eye contact with a straight face. This can be another way to "slide in." If this means he is looking for a relationship, you need to find out now. Don't play yourself and assume. Be direct! (straight face) You are too old to be gambling with your womb!

3: You want to know if he is local or from out of town. You need to gauge the type of travel involved if this is a thing you both want to pursue. A guy can have a whole "other" family or life in another city! It wouldn't hurt for you to fill up the tank if possible and go drive (up to 4hrs or catch a flight) to see his place if you are serious about giving him a shot! Don't be lazy, this is your future on the line!

4: You need to find out his living arrangements. He could be living with a female, his parents, grandmother, or roommates. Each living arrangement has its own implications for him, especially if he lies about it. It doesn't matter where a man lives, he needs to be honest about that sh**, if he is a solid man for you.

5: You need to know if he got access to other women he is seeing "seriously" while telling you he is single without any attachments! You don't just get a female's keys to her place, if it isn't serious to some degree, especially to the other female involved!

Don't expect a man not to be having sex with somebody, because he needs that to sustain his mental health. It's foolish to think otherwise, guys got different sexual needs. Don't disqualify him for that. Guys can separate emotional needs from sexual needs way better than you! Over the top religious people, beware! (smirk)

6: Does this guy have a job? You need to know how he supports himself. Does he have ambition? No full-time rappers or painters at this stage who are not making a livable wage! You need to know what type of struggle you are willing to have with this guy if he doesn't have a steady income stream. Is he going to be worth it? Is he lazy? You need a man determined to work hard to provide for his family all his life, if need be!

7: A man thinks about his future, and at this age, he should be executing some sort of a realistic plan. If he doesn't have a plan by now, he likely isn't going to be good for you and raising children to have a future. You are already late in the game with no children or solid relationship of your own. You don't have the time to mess around if he lacks vision!

8: Make sure you know the type of man that raised him, or he looks up to! It should be clear to you by now what his past has been with his father or lack thereof. If he can't talk to you about it now, he is a "sleeper," and you need to pass on him because he is too old not to have come to terms with whatever issues he may have had with his father in the past.

9: He must talk about the relationship, good or bad, with his mother, and you should know if his mother was good to him or not. You need to know how he views his mother.

You need to know what hang-ups he may have with her. A woman is the extension of a man's mother in the sense of how she gave him love or how she nurtured him. Whatever she did good you will benefit from that also. If she wasn't a good mother and or good nurturer, then you will suffer for that also, if not in the beginning, surely when you guys settle into a long-term relationship. A man without a loving mother can be a "cold piece" of work in a relationship! Look at my favorite rapper D.M.X. (R.I.P. 4/9/21) history with his mama abusing him growing up!

10: If this guy has had any type of abuse in his childhood, you will see signs of it once you are around him long enough. Don't take the small things for granted! They lead somewhere. You want to know upfront what has happened to him and if he won't talk about it. Don't waste your time dating him because you can't help him without going through the gauntlet of emotions and sometimes violence. He will need counseling, and if he isn't willing to work on it with a professional, don't even waste your time. He can drain you emotionally, financially, and physically.

DMX again proves true here. Trauma at home spills over into your relationships, then given to the children by your influence!

11: A guy that was adopted can suffer from an identity crisis and low self-esteem due to feelings of abandonment by his biological parents if he never received a loving surrogate family at an "early" age. Even still, low self-esteem can be an issue. You decide if he is strong enough to lead your family with much needed counseling before a committed relationship is even possible!

12: You need to know if this guy's early childhood was a good environment or a bad one. This is where his "character" was shaped. Research his environment on your own after getting some information from him on his experiences growing up.

13: You can't pick your family, but you dam sure can pick your friends! You need to know who his friends are. He picked them. Is he the leader type or the follower type? If he is the follower type you will exhaust yourself trying to guide him which is not your responsibility! You will only resent him, and this will bring you grief long-term.

14: By this time, he is well-grounded in what he likes and should have at least three types of music he likes. This will show his range of openness as a well-rounded man in learning and accepting new ideas to grow in greater wisdom.

15: His favorite song will tell you what his priority is in his life at the time. Ask him why he likes that song. The lyric of a song speaks volumes of what is on his mind and heart.

16: You want to know if this guy has the capacity to love. Has he loved any woman up to this point? If he hasn't, are you that special? You need to know if he is a good liar and doesn't have any plans for you to be special beyond the first 1-3 months of having sex with you, if that is what you allow. I'm not judging you. Don't be saying what you didn't know, before you give him the cookies, and you suffer later!

17: Does he tend to be violent? If he tends to beat women, you want to know now! You don't want to be a victim. A guy that has no self-control isn't a man at all. You can't beat a woman just because she said something you don't like. If you "beat" your woman, you are not a man at all, therefore will not be able to raise children effectively either! You don't deserve a woman. If he hit a woman just because she was sarcastic, then he needs counseling and likely they are not compatible for each other. We are talking about his woman, not a random chic who assaulted him. Even then, walk away if it makes sense to do so. Let's be clear. If you feel you got to hit a woman/man in the relationship, then it's time to leave!

18: Did he ever force a female in the past to have an abortion? You want to know if he is just irresponsible with his penis! This will show you the level he is willing to go and the woman's sacrifice for him. Did he make her feel like he wouldn't be a good father, so she decided to abort the baby on her own? You need to know something about his character.

19: If he has children, you need to know the age and if you want to raise another woman's children part-time or full-time. You also need to know what type of father he is now! Is he spending time with the children he already has? You need to know if he is open to having another 1, 2, or more, if that is your goal.

20: You need to be sure you know his temperament because this will ruin you if he is violent. He will likely physically and verbally abuse you one day if he has no self-control. Men have self-control to a degree. Males don't have self-control, nor do they feel for you in a relationship outside of what they want.

21: You need to know if he had trouble with the law. A guy that has been locked up had some type of issue, and you need to know what that was all about. This doesn't disqualify a man automatically, due to the nature of systematic racism, especially if it was selling drugs or small-time crimes before he was mature and other variables in his life! Perhaps, that is all he knew at the time, if this happened as a youngster! Get the facts first, and you decide! A lot of our brothers have been locked up for various reasons and scenarios. Does he have a felony(s)? Did he murder someone? Did he kill someone? You need to know if it was self-defense in the streets or is he just a scandalous type of person who hurt people for no good reasons! You don't need an un-reformed bad boy in your life, if you want a balanced and stable family life! They don't make good balanced partners in the long-term. His legal income is also affected because of his record. You must understand that if he has a serious record with felonies. He won't be able to get good jobs unless he is in the construction trades or runs his own legal business. Are you ready to carry the family economically? He had better be worth his weight in gold!

22: You need to know his goals and aspirations, if he has any! A goal-oriented man knows what he wants to do at this point. If you are dating men your age or older, he should know what he is working on at this point in his life. If he doesn't know, then how can he lead a family? There is a saying, if you don't know where you are going, any road will get you there!

23: At this stage in your life, you don't need any drama with illegal drugs. A guy is stronger than you physically, and if he has a drug problem, you could potentially be killed down the line by him or somebody he cheats who comes looking for him and they find you as well!

24: Let's be clear, if he is gay, that might be cool for openly gay men, but if you go into the relationship not knowing, that is a problem. It's not the time for you to find out after you have been intimate, and he is on the down low! Too many variables involved in you finding out after the fact. You don't have time to waste when you survived the gauntlet of dating to be over 35 years old without any children and in good health, just to get HIV/AIDS! You can get it other ways also, yet still be disciplined in your judgements!

25: A man that can't express himself at 35 years old or older isn't going to be a great teacher to his children. He may not be able to express himself in matters that a man is needed to step up. He will not be able to keep the communication going in a relationship with a woman where things will be misinterpreted at times. The best thing he can do is be a "quiet" example to his children by supporting the family with physical security and financial support.

26: Do you know what his belief system is? You need to know if this is going to be a problem for both of you. I assure you it is if you are unevenly yoked (don't believe the same spiritually speaking) with your belief systems. Debates on how you will bring up your children and lead your spiritual life should be discussed before you began seriously dating!

CHAPTER 13:

TRIED AND TESTED DATING EQUATIONS

"Opposites really do attract!"

"These equations just might surprise some of you!"

<u>Answer Key:</u>

Hyper-Masculine Man (HMM), Hyper-Masculine Female (HMF),

Masculine (M), Masculine-Female (MF), Hyper-Feminine (HF),

Feminine (F), Laidback (LB),

Passive 'Men Only' (PM), (E) Effeminate 'Men Only'

<u>Likely Results:</u>

*Unstable (U), War (W), **Likely Works (LW),

Abusive (A), Cooperative ***(C)

Best Possible Outcomes = ***

Decent Outcome = **

Struggling = *

(Man leading)

Man with Woman = Relationship Outcome

(HMM) with (HMF) = War | (HMM) with (HF) = (C) | (HMM) with (LB) = (LW) |

(HMM) with (F) = (C) | (HMM) with (MF) = (A)

(M) with (HF) = (LW) | (M) with (F) = (C) | (M) with (LB) = (LW)

(M) with (HMF) = (W) | (M) with (MF) = (U)

Woman with Man = Relationship Outcome

(Woman leading)

(HMF) with (HMM) = (W) | (HMF) with (M) = (U/A), (HMF) with (LB) = (U), (HMF) with (PM) = (A) | (HMF) with (E) = (A)

(MF) with (HMM) = (A) | (MF) with (LB) = (LW) | (MF) with (PM) = (A)

(MF) with (E) = (A)

CONCLUSION

I want to commend you for making it all the way to the end of my checklist! Again, I apologize to my sistas who were abandoned by those who should have protected them in their lives. You might be having some mixed emotions about what I said in this book, yet I assure you I'm showing you real love here. The majority of the younger sistas today seem to have been left to figure these things out alone in the Black Community. It's been a consensus that you have been taught that you can say and do whatever you choose in a Modern World created by men. God created a woman to be a man's companion, not as his *slave*, yet not as his *leader* either! If you don't believe in a higher power, then I don't believe anything I can tell you will matter to you. You will have to learn through trial and error, but if you end up alone in your senior years; let's hope you are financially secure enough to live your life alone in peace. You will not be happy competing with guys in a world where men will not tolerate another "masculine" image dictating to him how he should choose his marriage partner. I understand the delusional teachings that you have been taught and I realize you want freedom of choice. You have that yet look at the results of unwanted pregnancy and support for the majority of our sistas. Men will not change their mindset sistas, they will just choose another woman eventually if not at first! We know our time is short on this earth and most will not spend it with a woman that is not submissive to his leadership. Well, you have freedom to choose, but just before you continue ahead and lead that life alone without a good man, I encourage you to speak to women well past 55years old and see how most of them are living. See if they can sustain themselves in a society without other family members supporting them, namely their children or other women. You see instinctively men know, if we fall in the world, there will be nobody to pick us up, so we hustle our whole lives to ensure our security and that of our families. We suffer in silence and we push on as warriors! Most of the women look to the system in place in a 1st and 2nd world country to sustain them whether you are willing to admit that or not. Anytime there is a crisis in the country where all the systems break down, you see a glimmer of what our roles really are when systems that we all rely on fail! When a man doesn't have a family of his own, he is generally alone. When a woman doesn't have a man, she still has a support group of other females/women. Homeless women get abused and raped on the streets daily because there is no protection or covering! Evidence is all around you when you reject the rules of man, but it is undeniable after systems breakdown or warfare. Flow with it in your feminine nature, don't compete with us in the masculine sense. You won't win like that. A man has a duty to die for his family if need be and he is expected to provide and protect his family at all costs up until death! Society doesn't ask these things of our women for the most part. Doesn't that responsibility deserve respect while we are here, building and protecting the system that keeps you secure? I would ask any man and he would say yes. I don't ask males what they think because they know not the life of Men! I hope I've helped some of you with my wise words and experience. It is time to change our future, and don't be so eager to join the ranks of independence from the Black men that could possibly enrich your life. Social

Media is a great time waster for our sistas, thinking that time is in their favor. I can assure you with all in me that time is so short, from as early as you start having your menstrual cycle through until 35 years old or so; many things will come across your mind to experience, most of those things going from high school to the online experience with the opposite sex will not be for you to practice! Learn how to be a good housewife of a man, even more so than a college degree, if you want to be able to compete in this difficult arena with young females turning 18 years old daily around the world and joining the dating marketplace. I wish you the best in your decisions. I ask you to try the things I laid out in this book, even if you don't believe me and I'm sure the light will turn on for you in many ways, if you can be open to the information. You should be turning away ***most*** of the ***males*** that you *interview* with my checklists! Remember the rule for Modern Day long-term relationships which is 90% Males and 10% Men! God, Allah or the universe will bless your efforts, if you think twice before you let your ***emotions*** help you make *terrible* decisions with the opposite sex without ***consulting*** truly mature men and women who have a track record of happiness and or balanced *insight* based on *reality* and *experience*!

All Future Books will be available for purchase on Amazon.com, Audible.com, Https://AskMrWolf.com, BlackPeople.shop

Sincerely, Mr. WOLF

References.

BlackDemographics.com:
https://blackdemographics.com/

U.S. Census Bureau:

http://www.census.gov

Pew Research Group: https://www.pewresearch.org/

The Black and Brown Communities and Hoods of America!